金
山

**Also by the Author**
Arming the Chinese (*University of B.C. Press, 1982*)

# ANTHONY B. CHAN

金
山
# GOLD
# MOUNTAIN

## THE CHINESE IN THE NEW WORLD

NEW STAR BOOKS • VANCOUVER

First printing January 1983
1   2   3   4   5       87   86   85   84   83

**Canadian Cataloguing in Publication Data**
Chan, Anthony B.
Gold Mountain

Bibliography: p.
ISBN 0-919573-00-2 (bound). -- ISBN
0-919573-01-0 (pbk.)

1. Chinese Canadians - History.*
2. Chinese - Canada - History.  I. Title.
FC106.C5C49        305.8'951'071        C82-091309-X
F1035.C5C49

Cover calligraphy by S.M. Djao

Printed in Canada

The publisher is grateful for assistance provided
by the Canada Council

New Star Books Ltd.
2504 York Avenue
Vancouver, B.C.
Canada V6K 1E3

# CONTENTS

*For my daughter,*
*Lian Djao Chan,*
*a fourth generation Canadian*

### A Note on Romanization

Readers may wonder why names in some instances are followed by another in parenthesis. In the study of Chinese society, we are plagued by a variety of romanization options. Using Northern Chinese, or *putonghua*, is fairly straightforward: the *pinyin* romanization system is used. With overseas Chinese societies, many Chinese names and places are rendered in the Cantonese style. In order to integrate the Northern (sometimes called the Peking dialect) and the Cantonese for readers familiar with the *pinyin*, I have usually placed the *pinyin* in the parenthesis following the Cantonese. For common place names like Peking, Canton and Hong Kong, I have left these in their original pre-1949 renderings rather than use Biejing, Guangzhou and Xianggang. Sun Yat-sen remains the same, rather than Sun Wen. But Mao Tse-tung becomes Mao Zedong, the form now used in the People's Republic of China. Familiarity was the key to rendering some names in the *pinyin*, others in the Cantonese and still others in other forms.

# PREFACE

Chan Dun, my grandfather, left China and settled in Victoria, British Columbia, in 1887. He had considered Seattle and Chicago. Exactly why he chose Victoria, no one in the family seems to know. But we do know his options—whether Victoria, Seattle, Chicago, San Francisco, or one of a handful of other cities—were restricted to centres having Chinese communities. For Chan Dun and thousands like him, Gold Mountain—the New World—was those cities alone, not what lay between them. The boundary between the United States and Canada had no meaning for them. White stereotypes and myths about the Chinese, attitudes toward "oriental" immigrants, the pervasive hostility of the white world—these were basically the same in both countries.

There are some differences between Canadian and American Chinatowns, especially in their acceptance and use of the political machinery of the surrounding culture, but I have chosen to tell the story of the Chinese experience in Canada because it is at the heart of who I am, what I have become. The history of Chinatown is reflected in the history of my family: in its flourishing after Chan Dun's arrival, in its cultural and social life, in its support for Sun Yat-sen, in the fight against the 1923 Chinese Immigration Act, in my uncles' participation in Canada's World War II effort, and in today's continuing struggle against racial discrimination.

The idea for this book was born in October, 1974, when I moved to Peking for one year. There, I began to reflect on the irony of the fact that in China I was considered a Canadian, a foreigner; yet all my life in Canada and the United States I had been considered a Chinese. It soon became obvious that the Chinese tradition in Canada had never been explained by someone who had lived on both sides of this contradiction, who could bring it into focus. I believe that this process will have to start before our history in Canada can begin to rise above the realm of fortune cookie cliches and popular indifference. Here, then, is a Chinese Canadian insider's view of Canadian history.

In Victoria, Vancouver, Edmonton, Saskatoon, Toronto and Halifax, where I lived and worked while writing this book, I listened to many Chinese Canadians from many occupations and life styles. Old men like Chuck Lee and Deep Quong told me without bitterness how private firms had refused to hire them, not because the owners were "racists" but because they were "realists." New Canadians like Donald Chu, who spoke so eloquently against the racism in CTV television's 1979 "Campus Giveaway" program, told me in the same breath of his passionate love for Canada.

My inspiration for the book has been Angela Wei Djao of the University of Saskatchewan. She took time out of her own work on two books, on social welfare in Canada and on the working people of Hong Kong, to read my complete manuscript and to offer many valuable suggestions. Cheuk Kwan, who accompanied me on many excursions into media and community work, read part of the book. Paul Levine of Renison College, Waterloo, Roger Hall of the University of Western Ontario, Doreen Indra and Simo Nurme were other friends whose criticisms, interest and support sustained my enthusiasm for the project. Brian Evans of the University of Alberta allowed me to read some of his research materials on the Chinese in Canada and provided his insights into early China-Canada trade relations. Ralph Maurer and Lanny Beckman remained patient and understanding editors throughout.

Many thanks are also due to Professor Jerome Ch'en, Diana Lary and Peter Mitchell of York University, Professor B. Singh Bolaria of the University of Saskatchewan, and Howard Palmer of the University of Calgary, for their encouragement and support in this and other projects through the years. I am also grateful for the assistance of the staff at the Public Record Office in London, England; the Provincial Archives in Victoria; and the National Archives in Ottawa. Financial aid for part of the research came from a Saint Mary's University senate grant.

Sharon Kashton and others in the history department at the University of Alberta typed earlier parts of the manuscript. Linda Gilbert typed the final version.

Although this book could not have been completed without the generosity of my friends, colleagues and former teachers, all of its shortcomings are my own responsibility.

Anthony B. Chan
Saskatoon, Saskatchewan
November, 1982

# INTRODUCTION

The Chinese have never accounted for more than 1 per cent of Canada's population, but their role in Canadian history and society has been disproportionately significant. Unfortunately, this role has consisted largely of being the victims of racist abuse. Of all the immigrant groups seeking a new life in this country, only the Chinese had to pay a head tax—a fee for permission to settle in Canada. In 1923, the Chinese became the first and only people to be excluded from Canada on the basis of race. These early examples of institutional racism have been obscured by the commonly held myth that Canada is a "tolerant" nation, unlike, say, the United States with its "black problem."

This book is not primarily concerned with racial injustice. It is more concerned with describing the various aspects of Chinese life in Canada which have shaped a unique tradition and sensibility. In the areas of work, marriage, culture and politics, this study celebrates the accomplishments of the Chinese in Canada. But racism has continually intruded into the daily lives of Chinese Canadians and no serious history can ignore it.

One common definition of racism describes it as a "principle of social domination by which a group seen as inferior or different in terms of alleged biological characteristics is exploited, controlled, and oppressed socially and psychically by a subordinate group."[1] The Chinese arriving in British North America and Canada between 1858 and 1880 entered a land already conditioned by a tradition of racism implanted by the European empires as they sought to extend their dominion to the New World. The British view of the Chinese was reinforced by Britain's easy victory over China in the Opium War of 1839-42, which they took as proof of their superiority, racial and otherwise. It was natural for the British, as the dominant power in Canada, to enforce their prejudices in the realms of business, morality, social relationships and the law.

In 1884, J.A. Chapleau, the federal government's secretary of state, and J.H. Gray, a British Columbia supreme court judge, were named by Ottawa to a Royal Commission inquiring into the "problem" of Chinese immigration. These two men, who clearly subscribed to the widespread prejudices against the Chinese,[2] had to reconcile those feelings with the fact that in many ways Chinese immigration was desirable and even necessary—"a most efficient aid in the development of a country and a great means to wealth," as they themselves were to report.[3] Their solution was to allow Chinese immigration to continue but to recommend some restrictions to guard against its "least desirable" side effects. The result was the introduction of a series of head taxes. Beginning in 1886 (not coincidently, just after the completion of the Canadian Pacific Railway and at a time when Chinese labor was not so desperately needed), a Chinese immigrant had to pay $10 for the privilege of immigrating to Canada. This tax was raised to $50 in 1896, to $100 in 1900, and finally peaked at $500 in 1904. The head tax did not apply to all Chinese, only to those Ottawa considered least valuable. The law stated:

*11*

Every person of Chinese origin, irrespective of allegiance, shall pay into the Consolidated Revenue Fund of Canada, on entering Canada, at the port or place of entry, a tax of five hundred dollars except

a) diplomatic corps or other government representatives, their suites, servants, consuls, and consular agents,

b) children born in Canada of parents of Chinese origins and who have left Canada for educational purposes or other purposes,

c) merchants, their wives, and children, wives and children of clergymen, tourists, men of science and students.

No vessel carrying Chinese immigrants to any port in Canada shall carry more than one such immigrant for every 50 tonnes of its tonnage.[4]

The Chinese are the only ethnic group ever assessed a head tax for entering Canada. In contrast, during this same period British immigrants were given money to help pay their way across the Atlantic.[5]

Canada's political leaders were virulent in their contempt for the Chinese. Even though largely dependent upon Chinese labor to construct his cherished national dream, the CPR, Prime Minister John A. Macdonald said the Chinese immigrant

has no common interest with us, and while he gives us his labor he is paid for it, and is valuable, the same as a threshing machine or any other agricultural implement which we may borrow from the United States on hire and return it to the owner on the south side of the line...he has no British instincts or British feelings or aspirations, and therefore ought not to have a vote.[6]

In 1908 William Lyon Mackenzie King, then deputy minister of labor, said:

[That] Canada should desire to restrict immigration from

12

the Orient is regarded as natural, that Canada should remain a white man's country is believed to be not only desirable for economic and social reasons, but highly necessary on political and national grounds.[7]

After World War II, in his third term as prime minister, King's attitudes had changed little:

Large-scale immigration from the Orient would change the fundamental composition of the Canadian population. Any considerable Oriental immigration would, moreover, be certain to give rise to social and economic problems of a character that would lead to serious difficulties in the field of international relations. The government, therefore, has no thought of making any changes in immigration regulations which would have consequences of this kind.[8]

Such being the thoughts emanating from the highest political office in the country, it was not surprising that a steady stream of anti-Chinese legislation was enacted. Some acts prevented Chinese Canadians from buying land or diverting water for agricultural purposes. In 1884, a $15 license fee was levied to deter Chinese miners from prospecting for gold. Two years later, the same year the land tax was instituted, British Columbia forebade the hiring of Chinese for all but a few jobs.[9] It eventually became clear that the head tax was not a powerful enough deterrent to Chinese immigration, so Ottawa enacted a law in 1904 requiring immigrant Chinese laborers to have $200 in their possession before being permitted to enter the country. This requirement was over and above the head tax. In 1911, Hamilton's city council forbade the Chinese from opening laundries in predominantly white middle class nighborhoods.[10] After June, 1917, a Chinese was liable to arrest without warrant if a policeman so much as suspected him of having entered Canada illegally.

The Chinese were denied the vote in British Columbia in 1875, and in Saskatchewan in 1909. Ottawa denied them the federal franchise in 1920. These laws had the spinoff effect of banning Chinese from those professions for which citizenship was necessary—law, teaching and pharmacy, chief among them. Laws also prevented Chinese shopkeepers and cafe owners from hiring white women.

But the worst law enacted against the Chinese was the Chinese Immigration Act of 1923, also known as the exclusion act. Passed by Ottawa at a time when the economy was booming and the country was starved for labor, this act specifically barred Chinese from entering Canada. Even after the exclusion act was finally repealed in 1947, immigration policies continued to favor white settlers. The 1967 Immigration Act proposed to eliminate racial discrimination in immigration policies, but this did not prove to be the case. By 1975, Chinese immigration still represented only 7 per cent of Canada's total—an insignificant portion compared to the 29.4 per cent share of immigration taken up by American and British settlers. From 1946 to 1975, 4,195,700 immigrants were admitted to Canada, but only 2.9 per cent of them were Chinese.[11] The sentiments of Macdonald and King were no longer expressed by Canada's prime ministers, but they do live on in the application of immigration policy.

### The Chinese Laborer

Popular antagonism toward the Chinese contrasted with the attitudes of entrepreneurs such as Andrew Onderdonk and Robert Dunsmuir. They welcomed the Chinese, to build their railroads and to work their mines. But they paid their Chinese workers less than they paid whites. These payroll savings brought additional benefits. Hostilities arose between Chinese and white workers, generated by the differences in wages.[12] The conflict was deepened by the use of Chinese workers—chosen solely because of their race—as strike-breakers. A working class thus divided presented little threat to its economic masters. Racism and capitalist economic institutions proved to have a symbiotic relationship.[13]

There were sporadic outbursts by Chinese laborers against individual racist agitators, but initiatives against white industrial bosses as the instigators of racism were rare. It could hardly have been otherwise. Thrown into a new environment, separated from their families and isolated in remote work sites, Chinese workers were vulnerable to control by white bosses and their agents. They were forced to work in alien situations alongside strange people with different customs. As a result, these workers became dependent upon their bosses, as they were upon the compradores who brought them to Canada and now had also to supply their wants. The contract labor system clearly defined master and servant, boss and worker, superior and inferior, and it defined them along racial lines.

### Why Racism?

Racism in Canada did not spring up overnight with the arrival of Chinese immigrants. From Cartier to the present, oppression based on race is woven into Canada's evolution. When Chinese workers immigrated in large numbers to open the western frontier, they were greeted by an attitude of superiority among the white population.

Central to the idea of racial superiority were two notions, "manifest destiny" and the Hamlite rationalization, which became distinctive features of the British empire. In its simplest form, "manifest destiny" was the notion that proclaimed the destiny of the white race to rule the world.[14] Associated with this was a Biblical justification of white rule:

> Ham, coming late at night, entered his father's house. His father had been engaged in an orgy and lay drunk and naked on the floor. As Ham and his brother came into the house Ham looked at his father while his brother did not and covered his father. The story concluded with the statement by God that Ham shall have a "mark" placed upon him, his children, and their children's children, etc., and that they shall be servants of the world.

Over the years, the "mark" has meant non-white skin and "servants" came to be viewed as a legitimizing factor for the low socio-economic status of non-whites.[15]

The nineteenth century subjugation of Asian and African nations and the attempts to exterminate native peoples by European and American colonizers "proved" that the white race was indeed racially superior. At the centre of this "proof" was Social Darwinism, the societal application of the theory of evolution and survival of the fittest.[16] For imperialists and racists, the idea of natural selection was interpreted as a competition between individuals, nations and races. Those who survived were the strongest, more advanced, more civilized. The evolutionary process weeded out the unfit, weak, backward and savage. Social Darwinism "seemed to accentuate the 'scientific' validity of the division of races into advanced and backward, or European-Aryan and Oriental (Asian)-African."[17]

While Canada never became an imperialist power in the same way as Britain, it did possess a racist tradition founded on white supremacy. Because of the overriding influence of English institutions, customs, habits and thoughts, the pervasive attitude that Asians, blacks and natives were innately inferior was also part of the British legacy to Canada. With the vast influx of settlers from Britain, relations between Anglo-Saxon and colored immigrants were founded on the racial supremacy of the white race. Supremacist views were carefully nurtured and widely publicized. The popular literature repeatedly portrayed Chinese society as characterized by widespread poverty, loathsome disease, cruel vanities and low regard for life.[18] By contrast, naturally, white and British society was none of these.

The media played an important role by emphasizing the positive qualities of the white race as opposed to the "evil" traits of the Chinese. The Victoria *Colonist*, the Victoria *Gazette*, the New Westminster *British Columbian* and the Vancouver *Daily News-Advertiser* were unanimous in the view that the Chinese were debased and uncivilized. In 1884, the *Colonist* wrote that Chinatown was the repository of "all the combined waste from the laundries, saloons, restaurants and other places on Johnson and Government streets." It went on to say that the substance "oozing from the outhouses is the rankest filth, all combined rendering the atmosphere of the place so poisonous with stench as to be almost unbearable. The boards of the yard were covered with a green slippery slime."[19]

Despite their supposed inferiority and their alien customs the Chinese, according to the white press, somehow posed an incredible threat to white Canada. In a xenophobic frenzy, the *Colonist* warned:

> A struggle is coming beyond any possibility of doubt, and such a struggle as history cannot parallel. The tide-like sweep of the Teutonic tribes across Europe, before which the Roman Empire went down like grass before the scythe, will appear small by comparison with the advance of the Orient when once it has begun in earnest.[20]

The fear of an inferior and alien racial minority competing with the whites for scarce goods and positions blossomed into violence and brutality. There were beatings and killings in Lytton in 1883 and rioting, instigated by whites, on the streets of Vancouver's Chinatown and Japanese community in 1907. The imagined oriental threat was doubly worrisome to a population whose rights were inherent in their racial superiority. In 1900, the *Colonist* asked:

> Are we to have this great big province—a land virtually flowing with milk and honey—conserved for the best interests of the white British subject—English, Scotch, Irish, Welsh, etc.—or must it be given over entirely to the yellow and brown hordes of China and Japan?[21]

The view of the Chinese as inferior, foreign and threatening did not end with the introduction of the Chinese Immigration Act of 1923. Even though working-class Chinese were now excluded, a fear of non-white immigration still lingered. In 1931, Ottawa further restricted admission to Canada to British and American citizens and any non-Asian agriculturalists, and their wives and children under the age of eighteen.[22]

In 1947, 24 years after the exclusion act, the franchise was given to the Chinese. But with the founding of the People's Republic of China in 1949, the "Red Scare" came to dominate attitudes toward Chinese Canadians; the fear of the Chinese in China was translated into the fear of the Chinese in Canada. As late as 1962, *Maclean's* magazine could write:

> What Peking seems to want most today from Overseas Chinese is money—the foreign exchange they so badly need. According to one Allied intelligence report, the Overseas Chinese in 1954 were remitting $200,000,000 a year to their relatives in China...Between 1956 and 1958 Canadian Chinese, in bank drafts alone, sent more than $20,000,000 to China.[23]

The article also reported that the "laws that rule behind Canada's bamboo curtain are made by a criminal oligarchy with an immigration policy of its own." Its writer reasoned:

> Many Chinese born in Canada speak only a few words of English. Even those westernized Chinese who live in Caucasian neighborhoods are tied to the ghetto by business and social contacts. Most live and die in its confines. Few vote...They are the most unassimilated ethnic group in the country.[24]

Again, the Chinese Canadians are outlaw-criminals, foreigners and pariahs. Linked to criminal elements, they were a threat, as the writer emphasized, to "a free Canadian society."[25]

Chinatown the haven for criminals was not just *Maclean's* magazine's nightmare. On November 19, 1977, Peter Moon of the Toronto *Globe and Mail* wrote that many Chinese "immigrants or students from Hong Kong are involved in robbery, extortion, drug trafficking and protection rackets."[26] This article and one in the Toronto *Star* in July, 1977, caused a drop in Chinatown business as people avoided the area. In 1978, leaders of Montreal's Chinese community complained about the decrease in business because the area was pictured as "a dark and sinister" place.[27]

On September 30, 1979, on the CTV television network's program *W5*, the white depiction of the Chinese as inferior, foreign and threatening came full circle from the nineteenth century gold rush days. *W5* host Helen Hutchinson warned:

> Here is a scenario that would make a great many people in this country angry and resentful. Suppose your son or daughter wanted to be an engineer, or a doctor or a pharmacist. Suppose he had high marks in high school, and that you could pay the tuition—but he still couldn't get into university in his chosen courses because a foreign student was taking his place...Well, that is exactly what is happening in this country.[28]

Forming less than 1 per cent of the total population in Canada, the Chinese as "foreigners" were once again held up as a threat by white Canadians. On top of this came a 1982 Gallup poll which showed that 15.4 per cent of the white population wanted a white Canada.[29] Racism will take root in any society "that breeds an individualistic and competitive ethos. As long as building an alternative to capitalism does not seem feasible to most whites, we can expect that identifiable and vulnerable scapegoats will prove functional to the status quo."[30] This, then, was the "Gold Mountain" so many had fled to from war, poverty and injustice in South China.

# China Roots

Today Canton and its countryside, with its craggy mountain ranges and lush green forests and fields, is an important commercial and agricultural region in China. But in the days before the Tang dynasty (618-907 AD), China's aristocracy, accustomed to the arid north's dusty yellow earth, considered southern China strange and outlandish. When the Tang dynasty subjugated and colonized Guangdong province and its capital Canton in the eighth century, southerners were considered savages, a subspecies of the human race. It was where disgraced officials were dispatched; to be sent among these aborigines was a mark of ostracism. To help maintain order, the unfortunate official was given a garrison of rogues, foreign mercenaries, ex-convicts and soldiers, many of whom tottered on the edge of banditry and rebellion. Death was a certainty for many of these delicate, thin-skinned northerners, whose habits and constitutions could not combat malaria and other tropical diseases.[1]

But the northerners who survived these rough conditions turned Canton into a great centre for foreign trade during the

Tang dynasty. From India and the Spice Islands—Southeast Asia—came Persian, Jewish and Arab merchants with luxury goods for the Chinese upper class. Rhinoceros horn (a supposed aphrodisiac), pearls, coral, rare woods, spices, incense and agate became commonplace in the homes of the rich merchant, landowner or scholar-official. To encourage trade, the foreign "sea barbarians" were allowed to live, conduct business and follow their own customs and religions in Canton, Fuzhou (in neighboring Fujian province), Ningbo (in Zhejiang) and other interior cities.

The Chinese government controlled the overseas trade by placing a customs duty on all foreign goods entering China. Despite this, some "sea barbarians," through hard-headed negotiating and bribes to local officials, became rich and famous. During the Southern Song dynasty a grandson of the renowned warrior Yo Fei (1127-1368) was impressed by the wealth of one member of this new class in China, an Arab trader named Abu. He described Abu's home:

> There was a tall building several hundred feet in height, towering over a running stream. Whenever a visitor entered the building, he saw a golden plate underneath which an ingenious machine was hidden. Pressing the plate, he heard a musical, metallic sound. Going up, he noticed beautiful carvings around him, painted gold or blue, and sometimes both. Beside the building was a garden which contained a pond and a pavilion...and in its centre was a golden fountain. The fountain was covered with decorations shaped like the scales of a fish; I was told that thousands of gold pieces had been spent in building it.[2]

China's relations with Middle Eastern and other Asian traders were cordial. Trade flourished and both sides profited enormously. The arrival of the Portugese in the sixteenth century changed all that, and foreshadowed a much more significant change in China's fortunes. With a zeal for converting non-Westerners to Roman Catholicism matched only by their fondness for gold and silver, the Portugese exploited the hospitality of the Chinese. The Ming dynasty (1368-1644) opened China's ports to these new sea barbarians just as they had welcomed their predecessors. But the Portugese, once settled in South China and confident of their armed superiority, turned on their hosts, looting Ningbo in 1542 and Fuzhou in 1549. From then on Westerners were to be distinguished from the other sea barbarians—they became known as the *yangguici*, the foreign devils.[3]

Local militias expelled the Portugese from Ningbo and Fuzhou a few years later. (Canton, forewarned by the experience of Malacca, which the Portugese had entered as friendly and peaceful traders before seizing it in 1511, kept the Europeans at arm's length and was thus spared an attack.) But the Ming court, not wishing to lose the wealth which trade brought, did not entirely expel the Portugese from China; instead they confined them to Macao after 1557. Eventually other Western nations established trade with China: the Dutch in 1622, and the British fifteen years later, when three of their ships dropped anchor for the first time in Chinese waters.

In 1644, the Manchus—alien rulers from the northeast— swept the Ming dynasty out of China and became Peking's new rulers. They called their dynasty the Qing, meaning "pure." The Qing court, under the influence of Confucianism, looked down upon trade, but it desired the gold and silver it brought. The Manchus considered merchants a necessary evil, their existence justified only by what they added to the imperial coffers. On the social ladder, merchants ranked beneath artisans and craftmakers, peasants and the scholars who staffed the government offices. The Manchus, however, were determined to keep the highly profitable silk and tea trade under their direct control, and in 1757 they decreed that Canton would henceforth be the only port that could receive foreign merchants and goods. Canton was not chosen because of any Qing fondness for the city or its people. The decision was purely practical: Canton had the best port facilities.

Additionally, it was comfortably distant from Peking, the capital city of the dynasty. The Manchus reasoned: "If this evil is necessary, let it persist away from the seat of civilization [Peking] and in a southernmost city." The Confucian maxim, to respect agriculture and despise trade, was cast aside when trade brought great profit to the empire. Like all Confucian sayings, it was an ideal to be bent like the wind over grass.

Predictably, Canton during the Qing dynasty became by far the busiest and greatest trading centre of the empire. At the heart of the Canton trade system was a group of Chinese firms known as the Cohong. Because Canton was the only city made available to Western trade by the 1757 imperial edict, the Cohong had a monopoly on the import and export trade. It fixed prices and regulated how much tea, silk and other goods could be exported. In return for this privilege, the Cohong was responsible to the Qing court for the activities of all foreigners in Canton.

In 1759, the throne declared that "since foreigners are outside the sphere of civilization, there is no need for them to have any contact with our people other than business transactions whenever they came to China for trade purposes." But, "in an uncultivated, vulgar person, the desire for material gain is always stronger than fear of the law: this is especially true of merchants."[4] Regulations had to be adopted to ensure the harmony of the empire and the safety of the Chinese people.

The Cohong was required to make sure that foreigners left China during the winter. While in Canton, foreigners were confined to thirteen "factories," or areas, so that their activities could be observed and regulated. The Cohong also monitored the activities of their own merchants to prevent them from borrowing from the foreign traders. No foreigner was allowed to hire Chinese help for any services in China. To strengthen inspectional work and to keep the peace, the Cohong assigned policemen to the dock areas where the foreign ships anchored.[5]

The trade monopoly made Cohong merchants rich and powerful. The wealthiest of them, a man named Howqua, amassed 26 million Chinese silver dollars (worth 52 million

U.S. dollars). Part of his fortune was spent building a luxurious mansion staffed by 500 servants and ringed by a pleasure garden of "the 1,000 pines."[6]

## Commerce

By the 1830s, Canton's population reached half a million. Since it was the leading port in the Chinese empire, the city was a magnet for goods and people from all over China. Salt, fish, rice and sugar arrived daily from the Northern seaports on Fuzhou junks travelling down the Guangdong coast. Rice and cassia merchants used the West River to move their goods to Canton; these traders might meet junks from Yunnan carrying copper, lead, precious stones and gold along the same route. On the east coast, earthenware, tobacco, grass cloth, sugar, camphor, black tea and umbrellas moved in from Xiamen (Amoy) and Fuzhou.

Intricate fans and fine silk pieces with delicate embroidery arrived from Zhejiang. Green tea poured in from Anhui province, immediately west of Jiangsu and Shanghai. Hunan, Hubei and Henan, the central provinces, sent rhubarb, herbal medicine and drugs. Junks and sampans transported these goods from the interior via a network of lakes, rivers and canals.[7]

In Canton, the best artisans in the empire made fine toys to delight thousands of gentry children, and furniture to provide comfort for their parents. Members of the gentry bought jade, gold, pearls, cornelians, agates and topaz rings, pendants and necklaces from jewelry companies. Ivory carved in the shape of dragons, mythical deities or landscape scenes were also available to the rich.

Luxury goods flowed into Canton on Western, Asian and Arab ships. From what was later known as Canada came sea otter furs. Southeast Asian spices such as cinnamon, clove and nutmeg complemented the cuisine of southeastern China. Precious metals, jewels, cotton fabric and betel nuts also came from the Spice Islands. All these goods were shipped from

Canton by the junkload to other parts of China.[8]

Firecrackers, paper, mat-sails and cotton were also produced in Canton. Unknown to the Manchester cloth traders, Canton's cotton textile industry dated as far back as the Ming dynasty; more than 50,000 workers were employed in textile factories by the year 1400.[9] In the nineteenth century, a Western traveller wrote that 50,000 people were found to be weaving cloth in Canton.[10]

The only textile to rival cotton in commercial importance was silk. Nanhai and Shunde counties were famous for their black silk (still worn today by *amahs*—female servants—in Hong Kong). In 1819, these two counties, where many immigrants to Canada and the United States were to originate, had more than 15,000 acres of mulberry orchards providing jobs for several thousand households.[11]

Other workers could be found in iron foundries and gold and silver mines in the countryside. Fish, fruit and tobacco farming, as well as hemp and reed weaving, were other sources of income. In some parts of Guangdong, sugar cane surpassed rice in importance.[12]

Canton's booming labor market attracted the poor from the countryside; work was plentiful as long as the city was the centre of all trade entering and leaving China.

### Opium

By the late eighteenth century, Britain emerged as the leading Western trader in China. Tea was its major interest and was purchased, mainly with silver, by the British East India Company, which held the British trade monopoly in China. A cheap thirst quencher, tea was rapidly replacing gin as the national beverage in England; even among laborers in the countryside, tea was becoming the most common drink.[13]

By 1810, Western demand for tea, silk and other Chinese goods had poured almost 26 million Chinese dollars into the imperial government coffers. But the trade balance in China's favor was soon to tip the other way. The key to the financial turn of events that saw 38 million Chinese dollars leave China between 1828 and 1836 was what the Chinese called "foreign mud"—opium.

The highest grade of opium found in China was the Patna brand, grown in the British colony of India. Before the British East India Company began selling the drug to the Chinese in 1773, opium was used as a medicine in China. Because it is addictive, it was outlawed by an imperial edict in 1729, but Chinese port officials, bribed by the British, did not stand in the way of its importation. By 1836, more than 1,800 tons of opium, worth 18 million U.S. dollars, were entering Canton each year.[14] At that time, opium was the one, single commodity that could generate so much cash.

Addiction was so widespread by 1838 that a Chinese official lamented: ". . .opium smoking was [once] confined to the fops of wealthy families who took up the habit as a form of conspicious consumption. Later, people of all social strata—from government officials and members of the gentry to craftsmakers, merchants, entertainers and servants, and even women, Buddhist monks and nuns and Daoist priests—took up the habit."[15] By a conservative estimate, about 12.5 per cent of China's 400 million people were habitual smokers. Suzhou, a city renowned for its scenic beauty and landscape painters, had more than 100,000 addicts. The drug's effects pervaded social and economic life. Business ceased to function smoothly. Government service became more slipshod. The standard of living sank to an all-time low during the Qing dynasty because of the exodus of silver from the empire.[16]

The Chinese government was angered by the loss of silver and shocked by the decline in productivity caused by opium addiction. The situation worsened after 1833, when the British East India Company, the chief supplier of the drug, had its China trade monopoly abolished by the British parliament. The China trade was opened to anyone with cloth, cutlery or opium to sell.

Visions of a great Chinese market of almost half a billion

people excited the imaginations of British merchants. Here, it appeared, was a vast new market for the textile cities, Manchester and Liverpool. British capitalists were starry-eyed at the prospect of selling a pair of woolen socks to each Chinese, enough business to keep English mills running for generations (it did not appear to have occurred to them that the Chinese in the subtropical south had no need for woolen textiles). The China market was potentially huge, and dreams of vast profits titillated the minds of those Europeans addicted to profit-making.

China's efforts to stem the tide of illegal opium might have succeeded had Peking grasped an important but subtle change in its trade relations with Great Britain. Heretofore, European traders had been interested in the goods China had to offer—tea, silk, porcelain and other products—and China generously opened its ports to these traders. China neither needed or wanted any goods in return; it already possessed "all things in prolific abundance" and lacked "no product within its borders."[17] But at this time the British began thinking of China primarily as a market for its own goods.

The British wanted to make China part of its commercial empire, which had blossomed during the Industrial Revolution. To have a market for its cotton yarn and goods, vehicles, machines, ships and guns was the chief ambition of British capitalism. Ideally, these foreign markets would in return provide raw materials and agricultural products. With its 400 million customers, untapped mineral resources and fertile land, China was a prize, to be taken at all costs.

The navy was Britain's most powerful weapon for achieving that goal. Commercially-based and trade-minded, the navy played a pivotal role in the acquisition of colonies. By 1839 it had opened the way for its "nation of shopkeepers" in North America, Australia, New Zealand and India, and was ready to bring one of the oldest world civilizations into the capitalist system.

The sinking of three Chinese gunboats on November 3, 1839, began the Opium War. But for almost two years, the war remained indecisive. Finally on August 10, 1841, Sir Henry Pottinger arrived in Hong Kong on the British steam frigate *Sesostris*. Accompanying him was a navy that would eventually reach a strength of 25 warships, 14 armed steamers and 9 transport vessels altogether carrying 10,000 British and South Asian soldiers.[18] Pottinger's mission was to open China to British trade by securing treaty ports, abolishing the Cohong system and legalizing opium. By August 20, 1842, the war had shattered the myth of Chinese superiority. The Qing dynasty's elite Manchu banner soldiers, once feared, had become soft and useless during the previous three centuries of leisure and decadence. And its regular Green Standard Chinese soldiers and their matchlock rifles were no match for the British infantry's smooth-bore flintlock muskets either.

At one point there was hope that local militias could hold back the British troops. On land, mercenaries and untrained volunteer fighters were recruited by Commissioner Lin Zexu. On the waterways, the local boat people known as the "Tanga"—who smuggled opium on their "scrambling dragons" and "fast crabs" and supplied the British with provisions—were enlisted as imperial sailors. Chinese thieves were now being used to catch British thieves. There were also attempts to recruit ocean divers who could hold their breaths long enough to drill holes in the British ships. Hired killers from the secret societies and even trained monkeys were also enlisted in the fight.[19]

These desperate tactics failed to ward off the invasion of the British, whose navy proved invincible. After three years of bluffs, battles and finally the cutting off of the north from the food belt in the Yangtze River valley, the Opium War ended. The Treaty of Nanjing was signed in 1842; opium could now pour in freely, and the face of all China changed.

The treaty killed Canton's trade monopoly. The Cohong system was abolished, and Canton became a simple treaty port, with no advantages over four others—Shanghai, Ningbo, Xiamen and Fuzhou—created in 1842. Opium and the British shifted trade away from Canton to Shanghai and the other ports. Zhejiang and Anhui tea no longer found its way to south China. More than 100,000 porters and bearers and 10,000 boat laborers, who had carried the tea from Jiangsi over the Meiling pass and on to Canton, were thrown out of work. The Xiamen and Fuzhou trade to the south was finished. In Canton, dock haulers, warehouse laborers, money changers and the Cohong merchants all lost their jobs.[20] By 1858, tea exports from Canton had been cut to 24 million pounds from a high of 76 million in 1845.[21]

After the Opium War, British cotton goods became the most important export to China—next, of course, to opium. Many Cantonese textile dealers were driven out of business, unable to compete with the machine-made, far cheaper British cloth.[22] The cotton textiles stored in Cantonese warehouses rotted.[23]

Ironically, the Treaty of Nanjing made no mention of opium. The British wanted to regulate the drug trade by legalizing and taxing it, but the Chinese felt that legalizing it would imply their approval of its use. To ignore it was a way of dealing with that conundrum, and for the Chinese officials it was their one way of saving face.

From 1860 onward, 60,000 chests of opium poured onto the market every year, to the delight of the drug's users.[24] But the bulk of it was imported through cities other than Canton; the war had persuaded the Chinese opium agents to move their operations from there to Guangxi. Squeezed out in this shift were the porters, dock hands and river smugglers who had no way of moving *their* jobs from Canton.

In the countryside surrounding Canton, peasants living on subsistence incomes had to cope with the tax collector and capricious weather. Those who could afford the heavy tax that financed the war faced a drought that lasted from 1848 to 1850. Many impoverished peasants drifted into Canton to look for work. There, they would compete with workers from recently-closed silver mines, the many jobless water laborers and scores of other landless peasants.[25]

## Bandits and Rebels

Many of the jobless in Canton and Guangdong province were forced to turn to banditry or rebellion to stay alive. There was little practical difference between them; "respectable" society and the imperial government did not distinguish between bandits and rebels. Both were outlaws causing unrest and social discord, and both would be killed if caught.

In nineteenth century China, banditry was a periodic fact of life. Poor peasants, gouged by greedy tax collectors or crushed by natural calamities, would turn to robbing these same collectors as well as rich travellers, merchants and landlords. In China, stealing from the rich was a direct form of protest against injustice and exploitation. But theft never went beyond the merchant and official classes; because bandits relied on other peasants to protect them from the law, stealing from them was suicidal as well as immoral.

Not all peasants became bandits. Only the courageous, the able-bodied and those too young to have family responsibilities took to the hills and roadways.[26] Their raids were random and spontaneous, and they depended on an irregular spy system. Band membership changed frequently.[27]

Swelling the ranks of the peasant bandits were unemployed rural and city laborers and soldiers thrown out of work by the Treaty of Nanjing. These fighters, schooled in the arts of violence and plunder, were naturally inclined towards banditry; to the Chinese educated according to the Confucian philosophy of esteeming the civilian and the scholar, soldiers were seen simply as bandits in government uniforms. The Confucian saying, "Good iron is not pounded into nails, good men are not trained as soldiers," described the attitudes of many Chinese. To them, the soldiers' progression to banditry was not really a descent, but an affirmation of their normal appetite.

Just as the soldiers did what they did best in order to survive, boatmen, haulers and dock hands used their knowledge of the waterways to make ends meet. Following the Opium War, banditry and black market smuggling of opium, arms and other contraband increased in the waterways of Guangxi and Guangdong, the provinces most affected by the war.[28] In the late 1840s land and water bandits began to spill into Hunan. Near Pingnan, where the frontier areas between Hunan, Guangxi and Guangdong met, there were an estimated 10,000 Cantonese river bandits. A band of outlaws called the "cudgel gang" stalked the Hunan border, and the forest bandits of Tao Ba roamed Guangxi.[29] Recruiting unemployed laborers and hungry peasants, these bands sallied back and forth across the borders between Hunan, Guangxi and Guangdong provinces. The countryside became a militarized zone, a virtual fortress society where armed might was the sole arbiter, where there was no semblance of order or stability.

Bandit gangs in China were neither new nor unusual. They sprang up whenever the government was harsh, food scarce and taxes high—conditions that existed during times of war or dynastic decline. (One of China's best-known works of literature is the novel *Water Margin*, a tale of bandit guerrillas; the book inspired Mao Zedong.) Fiction romanticized the exploits of bandits, portraying them as Robin Hoods robbing the rich to help the poor. But this image was fantasy; the reality was harsher. With the British invasion and unemployment caused by Canton's decline as a major entrepot, many normally law-abiding people were forced into a life of thievery. Extortion, toll levies along commandeered roadways, kidnapping and robbery were common. But with government troops and bounty hunters on his trail, the average bandit could expect the executioner's sword. The poor and desperate, unwilling to risk their lives for the uncertain living provided by crime, began to look elsewhere for survival: toward Gold Mountain.

## Gold Mountain

As early as the 1820s, some destitute peasants and urban laborers were recruited in Guangdong and Fujian provinces of South China for labor gangs in Hawaii.[30] But only after the

Opium War did large-scale emigration to the New World open up. That there was a wondrous new land unfolding in North and South America was widely known in post-war China; this was of particular interest to the poor and unemployed, who were told that their ticket to the land of opportunity was an able body and a willingness to work.

One way to the New World was to go as a laborer bound to a contractor. But word drifted from California back to China, through clan and kinship ties, that there was a less backbreaking way of surviving, and even making a fortune. Gold—discovered at John Sutter's Mill along the Sacramento River in 1848—spurred many fortune-seekers to save for a passage across the Pacific in stinking, rat-infested clipper ships. Up to 25,000 immigrants from the Pearl River delta region converged onto the American gold fields between 1848 and 1852.[31] These were the lucky ones—pushed out of their own communities by the festering violence and chaos—who risked their lives in an alien and inhospitable world, a country considered by the Chinese to be primitive and underdeveloped.

Some did strike it rich in the California gold fields.[32] Tales of their sudden wealth spread swiftly (but not always accurately) back to South China; the handful was inflated into many and the riches earned became millions. America became known as Gold Mountain (*gumshan*) and was synonymous with hope, prosperity and stability.[33]

When the California fields were played out, the Chinese in the United States began to look for other jobs. They were joined by other Chinese miners, whom white prospectors had driven out of the few still-operating mines. Many drifted to San Francisco, where a Chinatown took root.

Then, in 1858, a second Gold Mountain was discovered in a colder and less hospitable climate beyond the northern border of the United States. Gold fever once more drew the Chinese miners, this time into the Fraser River valley in a country that would later be called Canada. The first nineteenth century Chinese immigrants in this territory were Chang Tsoo, a gold-seeker, and Ah Hong, a shopkeeper. Both travelled to

Victoria on Vancouver Island, the jumping-off point for the Fraser Valley gold fields, as soon as word of the strikes filtered down to San Francisco. Chang Tsoo and Ah Hong, however, were not the first Chinese to settle in Gold Mountain north. More than half a century earlier, in 1788, 50 Chinese artisans had accompanied a Captain Meares to help develop a fur trade in sea otter pelts between Canton and the natives of Nootka Sound by building a trading post, Fort Nootka, on Vancouver Island. After Meares was driven out by the Spanish, who were seeking a trade monopoly on the west coast, many of the Chinese crew decided to settle there, and sought shelter among the natives on the island. Later, reports from American sailors on the *Jefferson*, which was anchored at Nootka Sound in 1794, and from inhabitants at Fort Nisquallie of the Hudson's Bay Company in 1834, told of the Chinese workers mixing well in native society, making their homes as settlers, raising families with native women and growing old in the New World.[34]

These laborers gained a reputation for industriousness, honesty, hardiness and efficiency—a reputation that would be applied to succeeding generations of Chinese workers, who were seen as prized laborers with an added bonus: they were cheap!

### Popular Rebellions

The image of the sober, reliable, inexpensive Chinese laborer was enhanced by Chinese fortune hunters in California and British Columbia who worked mines abandoned by everyone else, and later took jobs scorned by white workers. Haunted by memories of the poverty left behind in a China torn apart by Western invaders, the Chinese workers in the New World became cogs in the wheel of capitalist development. But they had no alternative. Conditions in China had meanwhile worsened; returning home was out of the question.

The violence and chaos that resulted from the Opium War spawned a surge of peasant rebellions which initially brought new hope to the downtrodden and poor. The most famous of these was the Taiping Rebellion, led by Hong Xiuquan. A would-be scholar who failed the government examinations four times, Hong launched his uprising in 1850 from Guangxi; his allies were an ex-school teacher, a charcoal burner, woodcutter and another failed scholar. At the core of this popular revolt was a militant cult that worshipped the Christian God. Its followers were drawn from landless peasants, jobless miners and charcoal burners, poor *kejia*,* secret society members, bonesetters, smugglers, army deserters, geomancers, adventurers and river bandits.[35] Nicknamed the Long Hairs because of the long flowing manes they grew in defiance of the convention that men should wear their hair in long braids, or queues (a symbol of subjugation to the Manchus), the rebels developed an eclectic ideology which borrowed from Christianity, the folklore of the Zhou dynasty (1122-249 BC) and from the egalitarian and collectivist traditions of messianic peasant movements in Chinese history.[36]

The Christianity in the Taiping ideology was inspired by its leader, Hong Xiuquan, who in 1847 had collapsed in a state of delirium after his third failure in the examinations. He claimed to have had a vision at this time in which God entrusted to him the mission of liberating China from the alien Qing dynasty. Hong thenceforth declared himself the second son of God and the brother of Jesus Christ.

Taiping Christianity initially attracted many Western supporters. After Hong declared himself the Heavenly King and his Taiping state the Heavenly Kingdom of Great Peace (*Taiping tianguo*) in 1851, Western nations saw the possibility of a profitable relationship with this Chinese Christian movement. An Englishman named Lindley even recruited a motley group of foreign deserters and mercenaries to fight

*Kejia*—literally "guest family"—were nomads, an ethnic minority wherever they went, and victims of various kinds of discrimination. Wherever they settled they were considered "guests" rather than permanent residents.

alongside the rebels.[37]

But the Western dalliance with the Taipings proved fleeting. After the rebels had taken Nanjing in March, 1853, and declared it the Taiping capital, the movement spread northward toward Shanghai, the bastion of Western trade and commerce. The Westerners opted to defend the Qing court and the Manchus, because it was they who guaranteed them their rights and privileges. With foreign help, the Qing dynasty destroyed the Taiping stronghold of Nanjing in 1864. The captured rebel leaders either committed suicide or were decapitated. Over twenty million people died in the Taiping rebellion. It devastated the countryside in Guangxi, Guangdong, Jiangxi, Fujian, Zhejiang, Anhui and Jiangsu. The homeless, jobless and poor were more numerous than after the Opium War.

Other rebellions followed the Taiping movement. The suppression of the Nian uprising in central China, and the Moslem uprisings in Yunnan and Gansu, brought new suffering and destitution. Like the Taiping Rebellion, these uprisings were launched to free the peasantry from the tyranny of Qing rule, and their defeat led to new repression.

As was the case after the Opium War, many were forced into banditry. Others began to look beyond China for a solution. Southeast Asia, Australia, New Zealand and South and North America beckoned. The rebellions created a vast human reservoir of labor in China; millions of peasants and laborers sought a way out of intolerable conditions caused by foreign invasion and exacerbated by domestic warfare.

The railways being built to link east and west in the United States and Canada, meanwhile, desperately needed laborers, and contractors turned to China to tap that reservoir. The Chinese workers would be used to open the western frontiers of North America; they were to serve the business interests by building their railways and extracting their resources. Admitted as cheap, temporary laborers without the right to citizenship, the Chinese were, in the words of Judge Gray of the 1884 Royal Commission on Chinese Immigration, "living machines"[38]—labor for the benefit of progress and free enterprise in the two developing nations. They became part of a migrant labor system which was sanctioned by treaties imposed on China by the West.

# NOT A COOLIE TRADE!

Even in China, the self-styled centre of the universe, emigration was not an unknown phenomenon when the first laborers set off to find a new life in Gold Mountain. In fact, South China had itself at one time been a new world to many Chinese seeking a better life than the one offered in their northern homeland. During the Eastern Jin dynasty (317-420 AD), long before South China became part of the empire, Peking had to send soldiers to protect its settlers in the south from the tribal peoples they were displacing.[1]

The term *hua qiao* (the word *hua* means Chinese), used to refer to emigrants from China, gradually took on pejorative overtones. Much of the periodic immigration to the south and points beyond was caused by dynastic changes, when the generals and supporters of the previous throne fled to safety. It was not long before the very act of emigrating was cause for suspicion, and *hua qiao* became synonymous with "political enemy of the state." Why else, the reasoning went, would anybody want to leave the greatest civilization in history?

The Chinese government took its emigration policy to the

logical next step in 1672 when it banned emigration altogether, an edict directly provoked by a rebellion led by Zheng Chenggong (1624-1662), whose soldiers operated from bases just outside Imperial China. The edict stated:

> All officers of government, soldiers and private subjects who clandestinely proceed to sea to trade, or remove to foreign islands for purposes of inhabiting and cultivating the same, shall be punished according to the laws against commuting with rebels and enemies.[2]

In 1683, government troops moved forcefully against the rebels. Although the rebels were crushed, the migration edict remained in force. Remnants of the anti-Qing forces went underground, forming secret societies and other outlaw associations. Since many of these organizations operated in the countries of the South Seas, Qing officials viewed with suspicion Chinese travellers heading for those parts. A government statute warned, "those who find excuses to travel abroad and then clandestinely return home, if captured shall be executed immediately." It went on to declare that "those who smuggle abroad cattle, horses, ammunition, metal, etc., shall be whipped one hundred times." And finally, the government warned, "those who smuggle human beings or weapons out of the country shall be hanged."[3]

Chinese immigrants in distant lands, labelled as political usurpers by the Qing court, evoked neither the diplomatic protection nor the sympathy of Peking. In 1740, news of the Dutch massacre of hundreds of Chinese workers in Java was met with contemptuous indifference at the court. The government again declared that "those who have forsaken the civilized rule and have long settled in foreign lands should be severely punished according to the imperial statutes." As for the 1740 deaths, "since so many had been killed, it is to be pitied, but still they deserved what they got."[4]

## The Coolie Trade

The laws forbidding travel outside of China applied to the nineteenth century victims of the coolie trade—the seizure and sale of cheap human labor. The coolie traffic (the term comes from the Chinese word *kuli*, meaning "bitter strength") was a response to the West's demand for cheap, disposable labor, which had intensified with the abolition of outright slavery. America had abolished slavery in 1808 (legally, at least; slavery remained widespread until after the Civil War ended in 1865); Spain, Britain and Portugal followed suit in, respectively, 1826, 1833 and 1835. English, Portugese and Spanish bosses were especially eager to use low-cost workers to harvest their sugar cane, cotton, coffee and other crops on their West Indian and South American plantations.

There was no shortage of merchants, shipowners and others anxious to profit from the lucrative business of hauling human cargo from Asia to the New World. At first, the English plantation owners in the West Indies turned to such places as Penang in what is now Malaysia for their supply of labor, but it soon became apparent that it was cheaper to buy direct—to find workers in China itself. In 1845, a compradore,* contracted to ship a load of strong backs from Xiamen to the Isle of Bourbon in the West Indies for the French, opened the way for a stampede of flesh pedlars into the ports of China.[5] By this time the Treaty of Nanjing (which ended the Opium War in 1842) had cleared the way for Western trade, and the coolie traffic flourished. The competition for human flesh quickly became ruthless, as the profits were considerable and compradores were able to act with impunity, the Qing government turning a blind eye to the business. As was the case

---

*Compradores were Chinese who "served in a variety of capacities as intermediaries between decaying Chinese officialdom and foreign merchants. Their position was ambiguous. By shady methods they could accumulate great fortunes to live a life of cultivated ease. On the other hand, many Chinese condemned them as servants of the foreign devils who were destroying the foundations of Chinese society." Barrington Moore, Jr., *The Social Origins of Dictatorship and Democracy* (Boston: Beacon, 1966), p.176.

with the opium trade, the Chinese officially frowned upon the coolie trade (which they did not distinguish from regular emigration, still illegal) but were powerless to stop it, so they chose to ignore it.

At the Chinese end, local agents of compradores carried out the acquisition (by money offers, kidnapping, or whatever means necessary) of laborers and sold these to Western merchants, who shipped them to their destination. These agents were the processing cog in the coolie machinery, working closely with such coolie-exporting firms as Syme, Muir & Co. and Tait & Co., both operating out of Xiamen. Syme, Muir & Co. erected a pen in front of its offices to show off its fresh "recruits"; their business came to be known as "the buying and selling of pigs," and the pens came to be known as "pig-pens."[6] The principal in Tait & Co., one J. Tait, had a virtual monopoly on the coolie trade in Xiamen. Tait himself was the consul in Xiamen for the Netherlands, Spain and Portugal, three of the principal countries involved in the trade. A partner, Charles W. Bradley, was the acting consul for the United States, the other major customer. Finally, Tait himself owned a share in his company's largest rival, Syme, Muir & Co.[7]

In 1847, two cargos of 8,000 workers each left Xiamen for Cuba and Peru.[8] Between 1847 and 1862, American traders shipped 6,000 Chinese to Havana each year.[9] This huge demand for Chinese labor in the new world was met from the vast reservoir of unemployed workers created by the Opium War and the Taiping Rebellion. Poor peasants and destitute urban workers went to great lengths to escape their circumstances. Some were able to borrow or steal—some even sold off a daughter—to gather enough cash to pay their own fare to the gold fields of the Sacramento River valley or the Cariboo. Most, however, were not so fortunate. Few workers or peasants, threatened with starvation, could resist a coolie agent's seductive pitch: "If you follow me, you will get such good employment that very soon you will pay the small amount of passage money required and will save more than

$50-60 a year."[10] Some, however, did resist; these were simply struck unconscious and dragged to the pens like the one in front of Syme, Muir & Co.

Laborers were also sold to compradores by their own families to pay off debts, or as war booty from battles between clans or ethnic factions. Others sold themselves into slavery because of gambling debts, or were sweet-talked into selling their labor.[11]

In a typical case, a compradore or labor contractor would pay 8 silver dollars to obtain a laborer; in Santiago, Chile, he would be auctioned off to plantation owner, colonization firm or government for 112 U.S. dollars.[12] After the cost of the passage (estimated by American missionary and doctor Peter Parker to be somewhere between 50 and 100 U.S. dollars[13]), including feeding and shelter of the coolies and maintenance of the ships, was subtracted from the difference, what remained was the contractor's profit.

Crimps—compradore's agents—used any means at their disposal to seize prospects. In the beginning, the compradores paid them 3 dollars for each worker they procured. When crimps later demanded as much as 20 U.S. dollars per head, it was willingly paid by the compradore, an indication of the profits to be made.[14]

The Chinese people hated the coolie business, and it was not long before anti-foreign actions erupted. In 1852, Syme, Muir & Co. exercised its treaty protection and rescued a "pig stealer," or crimp, from a Chinese court.[15] In retaliation, local officials issued a proclamation stipulating that "from this time if any persons transact business with the Te-Ki [Tait & Co.] and Ho-Ki [Syme, Muir & Co.] hongs,* they shall be put to death."[16] Three years later, Prefect Ma of Xiamen proclaimed that the "abuses should be stopped." At Fuzhou in Fujian province, 1,825 workers were forcibly released from coolie ships. In 1859, four crimps were beheaded and an Anti-Coolie Trade Commission was set up in Shanghai.[17]

*Companies.

Antagonism toward the coolie trade was growing among the gentry. The Qing court, which had previously turned a blind eye to the traffic, was becoming uneasy. The abuses were mounting, and a solution had to be found. Finally, in 1859, Guangdong's governor-general, Lau Chongguang, legalized emigration for travellers cleared by Chinese officials.[18] Thus the illegal coolie trade officially came to an end; in reality, however, it continued because the Qing dynasty had no control over the other end of the business. It was not until the late 1870s, when Spain and Portugal agreed to regulate the worst abuses of Chinese immigration to their colonies, that the coolie trade actually ended.

After Lau's proclamation legalized emigration from China, Western nations seeking cheap labor began encouraging the immigration of Chinese. An agreement between the United States and China signed on July 28, 1868, was the most important international pact affecting the movement of Chinese. Anson Burlingame, formerly an American diplomat in Peking, was appointed by the Qing court to negotiate an agreement on its behalf. Without consulting his Manchu superiors in China, he signed a treaty which bound them to recognizing

> the inherent and inalienable right of man to change his home and allegiance, and also the material advantage of the free migration of aliens and subjects respectively from one country to another for the purpose of curiosity, of trade, or as permanent residents.[19]

With the most-favored-nation clause whereby rights gained by one nation having agreements with China would be conceded automatically to others, Burlingame's right of free emigration was also applicable to Britain and its former colonies.

### Free Emigrants in Canada
Like all other previous treaties between the West and China,

British accumulation of further rights in China by the Burlingame Treaty had a direct bearing on Canada. Its explicit free migration clause would provide cheap Chinese labor, not only for the massive railway construction projects uniting America from coast to coast,[20] but also for similar projects in Canada. Although the British colonial office by 1868 no longer administered the movement of people in Canada, Ottawa was still dependent on Britain in foreign affairs and thus benefited, as a most-favored nation, from the Burlingame Treaty.[21]

Under Section 95 of the 1867 British North America Act, Canadian immigration policy fell under joint provincial and federal jurisdiction until 1872. In 1869, when Canada included only Ontario, Quebec, New Brunswick and Nova Scotia, the first Immigration Act was passed. It allowed for a period of free entry in anticipation of western settlement and the final rail link to the Pacific. After 1872, the burden of immigration was assumed completely by the federal government.

The rights won by Britain in China as a result of the Burlingame Treaty provided cheap Chinese labor for Canada's national railway construction projects. In the 1880s, more than 15,000 Chinese laborers were lured to Canada by a contract labor system connecting Hong Kong and Victoria, British Columbia.

The contract labor system differed considerably from the coolie trade it replaced. Once a plantation or mine owner contracted for coolie labor, the Chinese laborer was kidnapped, purchased or otherwise procured by the compradore and his agents; the coolie had no choice of destination. Under the contract labor system, however, the laborer himself chose his destination—in this case, British Columbia—and paid his own way from Hong Kong to the New World. The role of his compradore in Hong Kong, the successor to the coolie agencies such as Tait & Co., was to advance him his passenger ticket for the Pacific crossing.[22] The laborer had to repay this debt, along with food and lodging costs, in an agreed time, usually from three to five years. The contract labor system answered a huge demand for labor from

North America as its western frontier was opened up. Soon many ships were sailing back and forth across the Pacific, carrying thousands of Chinese settlers to a new home in Gold Mountain.

The Hong Kong compradores were the principal administrative cogs in the contract labor system. They set up a network of depots in the Chinese countryside and cities to attract able-bodied workers, then processed them when they reached Hong Kong. No effort was spared to ensure that they were in good health when they boarded the ships waiting to take them to the New World. The agents' tasks included collecting regular fees from the North American contractors for the purposes of registration of laborers, and arranging contracts with foreign companies. In some cases, the compradores arbitrated between contending hiring companies for individuals.

The compradore, usually the sole contact between laborers in Gold Mountain and the old country, handled the remittances from the Americas to the workers' families in China, and it was not uncommon for cash to be lost in transit. Compradores also offered, for a fee, to ensure a workers' return to China once his contract expired, or to return his remains if the worker died.[23] This obligation was difficult to enforce, however, and was often ignored.

At the North American end of the contract labor system was another network of Chinese businessmen, known in the United States as the Six Companies[24] and in Canada, after 1884, as the Chinese Consolidated Benevolent Association (CBA). The CBA processed the workers upon their arrival, providing them with lodging, food and clothing. They also provided gambling houses, opium and prostitution.[25]

In 1882 Chinese workers began arriving in Victoria on their way to the Canadian Pacific Railway construction sites. During this period, all facets of the contract labor system had to be working smoothly; the CPR relied heavily on Chinese labor to keep costs down and profits up. The major labor contractor was Andrew Onderdonk, who had been contracted to build the British Columbia section of the CPR. Onderdonk would send word to contractors in Victoria that he needed a certain number of workers; they would pass the order along to their compradore contacts in Hong Kong, who would begin the process of lining up Chinese laborers. In 1882, Robert Ward, a commission merchant and shipping and insurance agent operating out of Victoria, responded to Onderdonk's first consignment order by arranging for 5,000 to 6,000 workers to be shipped from Hong Kong; they arrived in ten different ships. British colonial regulations stipulated that each ship be accompanied by one or more doctor, so Ward was able to boast to a Royal Commission on Chinese Immigration hearing in 1885 that "probably not over eight men, out of the number I had given, died at sea."[26]

The contract labor system demanded more accountability than the coolie traffic (which saw hundreds of indentured workers die of scurvy, malnutrition or flogging en route to the New World), if for no reason other than that the investment outlay was greater. The worker's value was also considerably higher because he had signed on by choice and was travelling as a free emigrant. After 1870, the contract type of labor was the only legal way a Chinese laborer could work in British colonies and former colonies.[27] Huang Cunxian, the Qing consul-general in San Francisco who was responsible for the Chinese in British Columbia, noted:

> The charge brought against the Chinese immigrants who arrived in British Columbia, that they are bought and sold as slaves, is not authentic. No Chinamen is permitted to leave China unless he does so voluntarily. The Chinese are employed and hired in the same way that the Englishman, American, Frenchman or German is employed and hired.
>
> There is no such thing as slavery in China and never [has] been as far as I know.[28]

The virtual slavery of the coolie labor system in the West Indies and South America never prevailed in the United States or Canada. Most Chinese headed for North America were signed to contracts specifying work and wages. Even the Chinese who came after 1858 in search of gold came as free emigrants. Unlike the workers contracted for specific jobs, the fortune hunters who braved the seas in search of gold were independent of the labor contractor. Their image of the New World was vastly different from that of the hired laborers. Dreaming of that one big strike, they were not restricted by bosses and low wages. In many ways, however, the miners experienced many of the same conditions that faced the Chinese worker.

# BACHELOR WORKERS

The trip from Hong Kong to Victoria took about 35 days under normal weather conditions. Depending on the quality of the ship and its crew, a one-way ticket cost between 15 and 20 Hong Kong dollars. A diet of rice, dried fish and preserved cabbage and other provisions added another 45 to 50 dollars. These expenses were paid by the labor contractors to the immigration brokers and shipping companies before the laborer ever left Hong Kong. Once the laborer began collecting a wage, a small portion, usually 2.5 per cent, would go to the contractor to repay the cost of his own passage.[1] Often, gold seekers travelled under the same arrangements as contracted laborers; those who were lucky were able to repay their fare with their first strike. Merchants emigrating to Gold Mountain sailed with their families in comparative luxury and at their own expense; often they would have had a hand in the labor contracting trade.

## Port of Entry
The first view many immigrants had of their new homeland

was Victoria's harbor. Before the arrival of the gold seekers, Victoria, lorded over by Vancouver Island's governor, James Douglas, was a quiet hamlet of 300 white inhabitants. It was a place marked by Sunday picnics, intimate garden parties and theatrical dabblings—attempts to recreate an English atmosphere.[2] On Sunday, April 25, 1858, Victoria's somnolence was shattered by the arrival of the *Commodore*, a wooden side-wheeler steamer, carrying 500 men from San Francisco.[3] Overnight, a tent village sprang up in Victoria.[4]

Douglas was not perturbed by the influx of fortune seekers; he saw them as a boon to the local economy and a source of revenue for his fledgling administration. By designating Victoria as the sole port of entry to British Columbia for gold seekers, Douglas forced all miners to detour through Victoria en route to Fort Langley, the major link to the gold fields. Without awaiting British approval, Douglas levied a 10 per cent duty on every import destined for the mainland, while products destined for Vancouver Island remained tax exempt. Further, merchants buying or selling goods in the Fraser Valley had to pay $7.50 a month for a trading license. Despite these levies, a substantial profit could be made selling provisions to the growing number of miners on the Fraser River: a barrel of flour would command $25 at Fort Langley, $36 further up the river at Hope, and $100 at the gold fields near Spuzzum. Prospectors also had to pay $5 a year for their license and $1 a pound for beans, sugar, salt and rice.[5] These high prices, entrance fees, customs duties and steep commercial taxes were the official welcome awaiting Canada's* first immigrants from China.

By the summer of 1858 Victoria was a cluster of tents, strung out in uneven rows, housing 6,000 immigrants. This tent town had little sanitation, no law enforcement to speak of, and severe food and housing shortages. By the end of that year, Chinese immigrants formed their own small community amidst this tent town, whose population had levelled off to about

*Although Canada did not come into being until 1867, reference to British North America as Canada before 1867 is used for the sake of continuity.

3,000. The press welcomed the new citizens. The *British Colonist*, founded on December 11, 1858, by Amor de Cosmos, the future British Columbia premier who quickly worked up a hatred for Asians, began referring to the Chinese community as "Little Canton."[6]

The Chinese in Victoria banded together for protection as a result of the mistrust, suspicion and race hatred that had been their experience in California. Chinatown quickly expanded around Johnson Street, where Jewish merchants, auctioneers and tailors had earlier set up shop. Chinatown's first laundry opened for business in July, 1858. Later that year the Kwong Lee Company—"Importers and Dealers in all kinds of Chinese Goods, Rice, Sugar, Tea, Provisions, Etc., Etc."—was established by a San Francisco merchant, Chong Lee, who later expanded his business to Vancouver. In the spring of 1860 the steamer *Pacific* brought Lee's wife and child from China.[7] Mrs. Lee was the first Chinese woman in Victoria, and her arrival marked the beginning of the Chinese family in Canada. The frontier Chinese family blended Confucian values with Christian teachings; these families were to provide stability and continuity in a Chinese community that was overwhelmingly made up of bachelor workers.

By the end of 1860 Victoria's Chinatown was augmented by laborers and prospectors who had arrived from Hong Kong in 1859, and immigrants who continued to stream into the city from San Francisco.[8]


### Men Without Women

By January, 1860, 1,195 Chinese gold hunters on their way to the Fraser River had passed through Victoria.[9] An individual like Chang Tsoo, the gold prospector, could stop off at Chong Lee's trading post and stock up on rice, tea, tobacco, silk goods, matting, clothes, shoes, opium and joss paper and sticks. For entertainment, he could head down to Fantan Alley and Theatre Lane, two side streets linking Fisgard and Cameron Streets at the centre of Chinatown. Too much entertainment could be a problem, but with the arrival in June, 1859, of Ay Kay, the first Chinese doctor on Canadian soil, remedies were available for physical ailments ranging from headaches caused by intoxicants to serious medical problems. From his office on Johnson Street, Ay Kay dispensed his knowledge of traditional Chinese medicine to all comers.[10]

By the spring of 1860 the Chinese population on Vancouver Island was 1,577. The rise in population would spark anti-Chinese sentiments among the 2,884 whites, whose numerical domination was dwindling. Women formed less than 1 per cent of the Chinese population. Even in 1902, when the Chinese population in Victoria was 3,283, the number of women did not exceed 96; 61 were married to merchants while 28 were wives of laborers, 2 had interpreters for husbands and 1 was a minister's wife. The remaining 4 had no occupation and were accused by the white population of being prostitutes.[11]

The low ratio of women to men was seen by anti-Chinese agitators as an indication that few Chinese immigrants intended to settle in Canada. If they did, they argued, their wives and children would have left China for Canada long ago and Chinese families would be the norm in Chinatown. But as Sing Cheung Yung, a Nanaimo market gardener, explained: "I have been here twelve years. My wife and two children are in China. They are eleven and nine years old. I would like to bring my wife and children here. She don't want to come. The people in this country talk so much against the Chinese that I don't care to bring them here."[12] These sentiments were echoed by Won Alexander Cumyow, who in 1861 became the first Chinese born in Canada.[13] A native of Port Arthur, British Columbia, he told the Royal Commission on Chinese and Japanese Immigration that "the Chinese have a very high regard for the marriage relationship. They usually marry at from sixteen to twenty years of age. Many of those who are here are married and have wives and children in China. A large portion of them would bring their families here, were it not for the unfriendly reception they got here during recent years which creates an unsettled feeling."

Alexander Winchester, a Presbyterian clergyman, reported that many Chinese saw Canada as their home. He told the Royal Commission, "I have met Chinese who had expressed a desire to become citizens, but claim they could not do so and maintain their self-respect. In explanation they said they could not bring themselves to belong to a nation that treated another nation so unfairly, instancing the unwarrantable attacks made upon Chinese in the press. Some Chinese who had become naturalized, hoping to bring relief from this treatment, had been disappointed."

Winchester, who at the time of his appearance before the Royal Commission was pastor of Knox Presbyterian Church in Toronto, also said that "there is hope of Chinese becoming permanent settlers if treated the same as other nationalities. At present Chinese allege that they are afraid to bring their wives and children to this country.[14]

Rather than expose their wives and children to the anti-Chinese hatred, many Chinese immigrants opted to remain bachelors in Canada for the rest of their lives. None wanted a life away from their families. But the profusion of racist agitators—like John Robson, editor of the New Westminster *British Columbian*, Amor de Cosmos, who became British Columbia's second premier in 1872, Victoria city councillor Noah Shakespeare, and F.L. Tuckfield of the Knights of Labour—all calling for more taxes, fewer jobs or straightforward exclusion based on fear of Chinese competition prevented the development of a social climate suitable for settling peacefully and raising a family.

Racism at the top emboldened those who preferred less genteel outlets for their hostility. A market gardener on his way to work could expect to be met with a volley of stones or name calling from young toughs and local neighborhood Johnny Canucks. Queue pulling, and taunts of "chinky, chinky, Chinaman" were almost daily events. No Chinese, then or now, has been immune from such street racism.

## Products of a Civil War

British Columbia, with its anti-Chinese feelings, was inhospitable, but to many, China in the 1870s offered little hope of even a subsistence livelihood. South China was going through a period of reconstruction following the Taiping Rebellion. More than 20 million people died during that war, which had lasted from 1850 to 1865; many more had been left homeless. In 1873 (the year the first anti-Chinese society was established in Victoria), South China was on the brink of ruin. For the poor Chinese worker or peasant, the choice was between leaving China or staying behind and perishing in the agony of poverty.

Southeast Asia, close by and less alien, seemed the most promising and congenial locale in which to build a new life. But an emigrant's destination was determined by district and clan ties. If you grew up in Fujian province, you were likely to emigrate to Southeast Asia.[15] North America was your likely new home if you were from Guangdong counties like Taishan, Zhongshan, Xinhui, Shunde, Haoshan or Nanhai. The racial hostility and economic uncertainty of Gold Mountain was usually preferable to the fate awaiting in South China.


## Labor and Wages

In contrast to the decades following the Taiping Rebellion, a laborer could still find work during the Taiping rebels' march northward to Nanjing in the 1850s. By going from one village to the next during harvest time, he could earn between two and a half and five cents a day. Those who were hired on permanently received three meals a day consisting of rice, pork fat, cabbage and rice wine. At the end of the year they would receive ten "stone," or about 2,000 pounds, of grain, worth about twenty silver dollars.[16] But by 1865 the fertile Yangtze River valley was "strewn with human skeletons, [its] rivers polluted with floating carcasses, no hands were left to till the soil." Another witness reported that many "have been driven to cannibalism to satisfy the craving of hunger."[17] For the

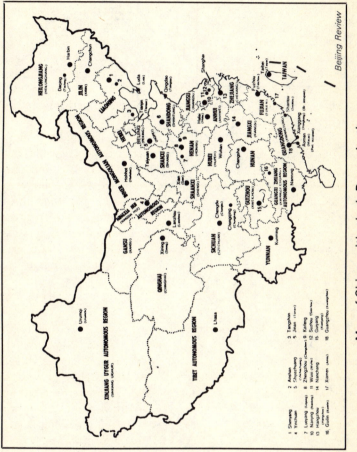

Map of China, with *pinyin* Romanization

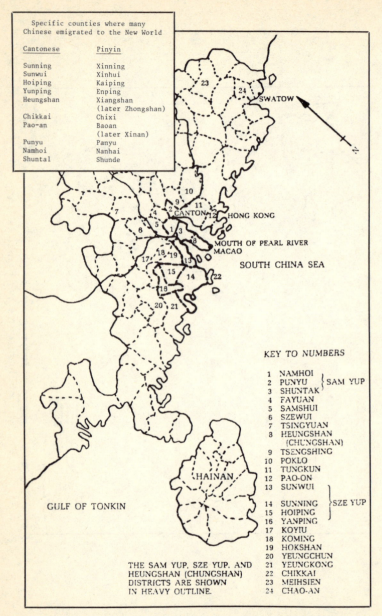

SWATOW

CANTON

HONG KONG

MOUTH OF PEARL RIVER

MACAO

SOUTH CHINA SEA

HAINAN

GULF OF TONKIN

KEY TO NUMBERS

| | | |
|---|------------|---------|
| 1 | NAMHOI | }
| 2 | PUNYU | SAM YUP |
| 3 | SHUNTAK | }
| 4 | FAYUAN | |
| 5 | SAMSHUI | |
| 6 | SZEWUI | |
| 7 | TSINGYUAN | |
| 8 | HEUNGSHAN (CHUNGSHAN) | |
| 9 | TSENGSHING | |
| 10 | POKLO | |
| 11 | TUNGKUN | |
| 12 | PAO-ON | |
| 13 | SUNWUI | }
| 14 | SUNNING | }
| 15 | HOIPING | SZE YUP |
| 16 | YANPING | }
| 17 | KOYIU | |
| 18 | KOMING | |
| 19 | HOKSHAN | |
| 20 | YEUNGCHUN | |
| 21 | YEUNGKONG | |
| 22 | CHIKKAI | |
| 23 | MEIHSIEN | |
| 24 | CHAO-AN | |

THE SAM YUP, SZE YUP, AND
HEUNGSHAN (CHUNGSHAN)
DISTRICTS ARE SHOWN
IN HEAVY OUTLINE.

Guangdong (Kwangtung) province, showing the counties
where most Chinese immigrants to Gold Mountain originated

Howqua, a leading Hong merchant

The curse of opium: an addict threatens his wife and mother.
A popular depiction from the 1920s

British troops near Canton during the Opium War

Fantan Alley in decay, 1978

many Chinese struggling against starvation, the call for men to build railways in North America was difficult to resist, and those who were still able signed on for the transpacific voyage. From 1876 to 1880, 3,326 immigrants arrived in Victoria; in 1885, six ships from Hong Kong brought 1,739 passengers. Not all of these laborers were able to start work immediately; about 10 per cent had developed scurvy, caused by poor food and lack of ventilation on board ship. Because of the raging seas and stormy weather, the Chinese were kept below deck with the hatches bolted.

The workers who arrived in British Columbia from the United States by land were in much better health because they were not subjected to a transpacific voyage. Adding to the Hong Kong total were 387 from the Puget Sound area and another 387 from San Fancisco. During the entire five-year construction period, about 15,000 rail hands were hired by Andrew Onderdonk to build the tracks linking British Columbia with the rest of Canada.[18]

Unlike the independent gold hunters of 1858, the Chinese laborers from the United States were under contract to Chinese compradores in San Francisco. The compradores originated in China's treaty ports after the Opium War in 1842, when they had been hired by foreign trading houses in China to deal with the Chinese side of their business. Usually bilingual, they acted as intermediaries between the foreign merchant and the huge Chinese domestic market. In the Americas, the compradores still functioned as go-betweens, but they were often independent of any foreign control.

The most active compradore firms in securing railway workers were the companies of Lian Chang, Tai Chong and Lee Chuck. Their Victoria offices became the final stop-off point for all of the workers contracted out of San Francisco and Hong Kong.

Immigration brokerage, however, was in white hands. In June, 1881, most of the 6,676 laborers arriving from Hong Kong were consigned to non-Chinese immigration brokers—5,297 to the firm of Stahlschmidt & Ward, and 450 to Welch &

Rithet.[19] The only Chinese company able to compete with the white brokers was Lian Chang, through its contracts with Onderdonk for 2,000 workers in 1881. Much of the profit from the trade in Chinese muscle during this time did not go into the coffers of the compradores.

Because labor brokers' profits depended on workers arriving in Canada in good health, the ships carrying Chinese workers upgraded their food and living conditions after 1882. The *Colonist* reported that on November 15, 1881, the *Volmer* arrived in Victoria with "224 Chinese who had been aboard for 50 days. They lived on a pound and a half of rice, a half pound of meat, and a half pound of vegetables per man per day, with an allowance of fruit or lime juice."[20] Because their strong backs were needed to fulfil John A. Macdonald's pledge to unite Canada by rail, Chinese laborers were temporarily indulged.

## Boss Onderdonk

The Chinese role in the construction of the Canadian Pacific Railway began at eleven in the morning on May 14, 1880, with the firing of a blasting cap near Yale, British Columbia. Central to the working lives of all the Chinese employed on the rail line was Andrew Onderdonk, whose imposing presence dominated the British Columbia chapter of the CPR story. A civil engineer by trade, his towering figure commanded such respect among even the white laborers that they would tip their caps when he passed by on the railroad.

A reserved and detached figure who was always impeccably dressed in the latest Wall Street fashions, Onderdonk was the ideal contractor for the CPR's stretch run to the Pacific. His experience in the United States—by age 37 he had already organized the construction of San Francisco's seawall and ferry boats—revealed him as an efficient, no-nonsense achiever whose only interest besides the task at hand was profits.[21] Like many other employers, Onderdonk imported Chinese muscle because he believed that "99 per cent of the Chinese here are industrious and steady" and that the "development of the country would be retarded and many industries abandoned" if Chinese laborers were not allowed to work in North America.[22] Onderdonk eagerly sought compradores who could ferret Chinese workers out of the decaying corners of the streets of Hong Kong and the market gardens and laundries of San Francisco.

Their reputation as the best labor money could buy started with the building of the Central Pacific Railway in the United States. Gathered together by Charles Crocker, the Central Pacific's labor contractor, the Chinese were hired to supplement the Irish-American rail hands. It started as an experiment involving 50 unemployed miners, laundry workers, market gardeners, domestic servants and laborers. After seeing the cleanliness of the Chinese camp, their ability to adapt to the thin air of the Sierras, and their toughness in handling a pick and shovel, Crocker hired 6,000 more by 1866 at $35 a month (board and lodging were not supplied; white workers received board and lodging in addition to their pay of about a dollar a day). During its most hectic period of construction, between 1866 to 1869, the Central Pacific obtained about 90 per cent of its 10,000 rail hands from the Chinese labor market, thereby saving itself $5.5 million.[23]

By the time Onderdonk began laying tracks for the Northern Pacific in Oregon in 1880 and the Southern Pacific in California in 1881, the Chinese rail hand had earned a reputation as the most able and least expensive worker available. Sir Mathew Begbie, the British Columbia chief justice, declared that the four personal qualities of the Chinese were "industry, economy, sobriety, and law-abidingness."[24] And J.A. Chapleau, a cabinet minister of the Conservative Canadian government who along with J.J.C. Abbott and Joseph Tasse had incorporated the 88-mile Montreal and Western Railway and later sold it to the CPR, wrote in 1885 that the Chinese worker had "no superior as a railway navvy." He also noted that the money saved by paying the Chinese lower wages than whites found its way into the profit ledger of railway companies.[25] Perhaps the most famous endorsation of the Chinese laborer was made by Prime Minister John A. Macdonald, who in 1882 told parliament that although the Chinese were "alien" and would never assimilate into the "Aryan" way of life, stressed that "it is simply a question of alternatives: either you must have this labor or you can't have the railway."[26]

Politicians and railway investors grudgingly admitted that the Chinese worker was valuable and even necessary, a conclusion based almost entirely on dollars and cents. When profits and savings on wages motivate the builders of the country, they tend to become color-blind.

Virulent attacks on the Chinese worker came from the Knights of Labour, an early organization of skilled workers, which attacked the Chinese "as a low, degraded and servile type, the inevitable result of whose employment in competition with free white labor is to lower and degrade the latter without any appreciable elevation of the former." Competition, however, was not the main objection. Rather, the Chinese were "the willing tools whereby grasping and tyrannical employers grind down all labor to the lowest living point."[27]

If there was any degradation in the value of white workers because of the hiring of the Chinese, it did not show up in their pay envelope or accommodations. In April, 1880, Onderdonk assured the Anti-Chinese Society that white workers would always be given preference in hiring; once this labor pool was exhausted, he would turn to French Canadians and finally he would "with reluctance, engage Indians and Chinese." Consequently, according to Onderdonk's engineer Henry Cambie, unemployed clerks, "broken-down bar-keepers or one of that class" as well as "rough-necks" and "sand-lot hoodlums" from San Francisco were given higher wages and better camps than Chinese.[28] Onderdonk paid his white laborers $1.50 to $1.75 a day, and a skilled worker got between $2 and $2.50 per day. He also provided cooks, cooks' helpers and other amenities to accommodate the taste of his white employees.

In contrast, Chinese workers all received the same wage—$1 per day, regardless of the work they performed. For provisions, they were given a choice between inflated prices at the company stores and competitive prices at local trading houses, if there were any nearby. They had to buy their own provisions, bringing their daily wage down to 80 cents. There were other expenses too. The Chinese laborer, unlike his white counterpart, had to dig into his own pocket for camping equipment and cooking items. Chinese rail hands would travel light, carrying all of their needs on their backs. They could quickly break camp, trek as far as 25 miles and set up a new camp within 24 hours. According to Michael Haney, Onderdonk's general manager, 2,000 Chinese laborers could be moved such a distance within a complete day. The same number of white laborers needed about a week to move camp. The advantages of Chinese mobility did not escape Onderdonk's attention.[29]

It was not the Chinese who were responsible for the white workers' low standards of living; it was Onderdonk, and bosses like him, who decided the pay structure and living arrangements for both white and non-white workers. Compared to the Chinese, white laborers were pampered, getting better wages and housing. But the white rail hand in British Columbia was getting 25 cents less per day than his American counterpart, and skilled white laborers for American railways received $1 a day more than did Canadian skilled workers. Beside the discrepancy in wages, Onderdonk's workers had to lay tracks on difficult terrain, in mountainous areas and alongside fast-rising rivers, in areas where the population was sparse and unsettled.[30]

Onderdonk's section of the CPR was bankrolled by American tycoons, mostly bankers. They included Darius O. Mills, H.B. Laidlaw, Levi P. Morton and S.G. Reed of the Oregon Railway and Navigation Company. Because of Onderdonk's family connections he was privy to the board rooms of the eastern establishment in the United States. Since the prime objective of this bankers' syndicate was maximum profit, Onderdonk had to secure majority interest in, or complete control of, the British Columbia rail route. Fortunately for him and his bankers, the Canadian government had a policy of encouraging private construction in certain areas of the country. Land grants and a large sum of cash subsidies sweetened the taste for railway construction west of Winnipeg.[31]

Onderdonk had to eliminate equally avaricious rivals to win the contracts for the British Columbia section of the CPR. In his tenders for the four contracts involved, well-placed friends and allies in Ottawa saw to it that even the lowest bidders had little chance of success. Among Onderdonk's Ottawa friends was Charles Tupper, who as Canada's minister of railways had to cope with the failures of badly financed railway contractors. Recognizing the financial power of Onderdonk's American connection, Tupper supported his bid for the four British Columbia contracts.

Beyond patronage, a successful bid depended on an impressive track record, experience in labor relations and the ability to balance the books. In all these aspects, Onderdonk's company was the best of the competition. More importantly for Onderdonk, Tupper was inclined to award the four contracts to one firm, thus sparing Ottawa from dealings with more than one company. Onderdonk's monopoly on railway construction gave him *carte blanche* in the buying of labor and materials, a powerful bargaining position with British Columbia politicians and anti-Chinese racists. The bureaucratic efficiency that went with needing only one paymaster and merchant, one time table and work schedule, and one arbiter and boss, added to Onderdonk's power.

His 1880 contracts covered the lower Fraser and main Thompson rivers, east and west of Lytton. It included the entire 127 miles from Emory's Bar at the mouth of the Fraser Canyon to Savona's Ferry near Kamloops. In 1882, the government also awarded Onderdonk the Emory's Bar-Port Moody entension.[32]

### The "Chinese" Pacific Railway

The 15,000 Chinese laborers who worked for Onderdonk between May 14, 1880, and completion of the railway on July 29, 1885, saved his company $3-5 million.[33] At first, they were organized into mobile gangs of 30 workers, lorded over by a white overseer, or herder. Later, when they settled into camps, a cook, a cook's helper and a bookman were assigned to each gang. The bookman was responsible for collecting the wages from the company and paying them to the workers, and representing his gang to the employer. His most immediate contact with the railway company was the herder, Onderdonk's representative at the grass roots level. Another task of the bookman was to buy provisions for the workers at the lowest possible price.

Because of the salary differences, the Chinese laborers usually lived on a monotonous diet of rice and stale ground salmon while his white counterpart ate fresh meat and vegetables. The result was a growing list of scurvy victims, unable to receive medical help in the camps. No doctors or medicine were available for the workers; compradore firms knew that such services cost money and would do nothing to enhance their profits. As long as unemployment in China was severe, human muscle was readily available.

The construction company, too, was indifferent to the workers' health needs; Onderdonk benevolently refused to interfere in Chinese affairs. The sick, injured or dying lived either in the same bunkhouses in the permanent Chinese camps or in segregated tents along the construction line. Entertainment was limited to fantan and other gambling activities. A total of 15,000 Chinese worked on Onderdonk's railway but only 7,000 were on his payroll at any one time, so turnover among the rail hands was high, and news of China and Chinese communities in Canada circulated freely and rapidly.

Some Chinese laborers supplemented their income by selling to the white workers a potent homebrew known as "Chinese gin."[34] But generally Chinese contact with whites and native

Indians was minimal; each crew lived and worked by an unwritten rule of segregation. Most Chinese workers communicated with whites only through their bookman, if at all. Knowledge of the English language was not a necessity and there was little incentive to learn it. Even if a Chinese did want to learn the language, English teachers were hard to find at a railway construction site. There was the bookman, but he had no interest in teaching other Chinese English; his knowledge of English gave him access to the white world, and, as the major intermediary between the white and Chinese worlds, a position of power in the latter. A white rail hand, because of his antipathy toward his Chinese colleague, was as likely to teach a Chinese English as he was himself inclined to learn Chinese.

## Divide and Rule

The tense, suspicious relations between the races prevented understanding and respect between Chinese and white workers. Company bosses never spoke of using these racial differences as an instrument of control, but racial animosity did prevent Chinese and whites from joining together into an effective union that could demand fair wages, better housing and job safety. In the absence of such a union, Onderdonk and his syndicate profited from the racial differences. They kept Chinese wages low, but not so low that they did not infuriate white workers. Vital to Onderdonk's policy of divide and rule was the constant flow of anti-Chinese propaganda thrown at the white laborer by journalists like John Robson, politicians like Amor de Cosmos and Noah Shakespeare, and labor leaders like F.L. Tuckfield. Focusing on the Chinese as a foreign threat to the "free" white labor market helped to deflect grievances white workers might have against their bosses. The propagandists, whose interest was supposedly in the betterment of white labor, emphasized that each successful Chinese meant the failure of one white worker. But Onderdonk was not beloved by them either, even though he did benefit from their invectives; they opposed the hiring of Chinese rail hands.

For some like Noah Shakespeare, involvement in racist organizations like the Anti-Chinese Society was a tool for their own political advancement. Shakespeare's election pledge to rid Canada of the Chinese menace brought him the mayoralty of Victoria and a seat in parliament in Ottawa. Because the political flavor of the times was so anti-Asian, no politician with ambitions could risk dissociating himself from racist views. Like the white workers, politicians attacked everything Chinese—dress, speech, customs, pay packages, etc. They preyed on the insecurities of the white laborer, harping on the "strangeness" of the Chinese. They pointed to his cotton shoes, his Chinese-style workers jacket with cloth buttons, and his loose cotton trousers. But they failed to point to his meagre wages, which prevented a Chinese rail hand from buying expensive Western apparel, should he wish to do so.

## A "Chinaman's Chance"

The work assigned to Chinese laborers was the most back-breaking and dangerous on the railway. Initially, the Chinese were assigned to the task of grading—cutting out hills to fill ravines and gullies. Later, the more dangerous jobs of tunneling and the handling of explosives were given to the Chinese. It was they who opened the frontier for the white rail hands who were responsible for the lumber work, for the construction of bridges and tunnels and the laying of track.

Conflicts between Chinese and white workers were not infrequent. In August, 1880, a dynamite explosion near Yale killed or maimed nine Chinese laborers standing on a rock directly below the charge. No warning had been given by the white herder, who claimed the Chinese had misunderstood his orders. An angry, pick-wielding group of Chinese rail hands forced the terrified herder to scramble to safety up the side of a hill. No inquiry was convened to investigate this incident. From this and similar events, the Chinese came to realize that the concepts of justice and fair play, so praised by the English, did not apply to them.

In another incident, several Chinese asked the overseer for permission to light a fire to boil water for tea along the line. His refusal so angered them that the entire gang threw down their picks and shovels and left for Yale.

Sometimes clashes between Chinese and whites resulted in bloodshed. Once, a herder tried to fire two Chinese without consulting their bookman. This disagreement exploded into an attack by the Chinese work gang on the foreman, bridge superintendent, time keeper and a teamster; a retaliatory night raid by white workers left the Chinese bunkhouse burnt to the ground and several Chinese beaten. One died the next day.

The bookman who led his workers' protests against any pay deductions was a powerful individual. Once, in the early days of construction at Yale, the Chinese found that their pay packages were a penny an hour short. After a long and heated discussion in the company's stores, the "mistake" was admitted and the money was paid.

However, the bookman was not always on the workers' side. At times he was the object of the enmity of his workers, as when they suspected that he had pocketed part of their wages. In one such occurrence, a bookman was attacked for cheating his workers during the building of the Grand Trunk Railway to Hope in 1874.

Chinese laborers would also take on Chinese companies if they thought they had been cheated. One time, the trading company belonging to Lee Chuck had agreed to supply rice for the workers outside Yale. On the day of delivery, the workers discovered that the agreed-upon price had been raised to include a 2 per cent deduction from their salaries. The unauthorized increase, as well as a deficiency in the quality and weight of the cargo, drove 200 laborers to storm and destroy Lee Chuck's warehouse in Yale.[35]

Many Chinese deaths resulted either from premeditated negligence or simple incompetence on the part of the herders, other white laborers or the company itself. Failure to warn Chinese rail hands of imminent explosions, inadequate protection from falling boulders and rock slides, and the lack of safety precautions against cave-ins gave rise to the saying in Canada's Chinatowns that "for every foot of railroad through the Fraser Canyon, a Chinese worker died." At least 600 laborers gave up their lives so that John A. Macdonald's dream of a Canada united from coast to coast could be realized.[36] Even in death, the Chinese could be worth money; an Irish entrepreneur named Big Mouth Kelly was able to secure a monopoly on burying the Chinese dead.[37]

## Labor Used, Labor Discarded

Completion of the CPR forced thousands of Chinese to migrate across Canada in search of work. The trek eastward was caused in part by Andrew Onderdonk's refusal to honor his pledge to provide railhands with a one-way ticket back to China.[38] Many laborers were left destitute and stranded in a foreign land.

The art of saving their meagre wages taxed the mental agility of even the most frugal, especially when the typical salary of a Chinese worker was $25 per month. Because typically there was no work for three months each winter, his annual income would be $225. From this had to be deducted, $130 for provisions and clothing, $24 for room rent, $10 for tools and transportation, $5 for revenue and road taxes, $5 for religious fees, $3 for doctors and medicine (if they were available), and $5 for oil, light and tobacco. That left a grand total of $43 for everything else.[39] A worker toiling for five years on the Onderdonk section could have saved $215; food and passage back to China cost $70. But those who were able to save even that were few; most ended up, as the *Island Sentinel* reported, "in the old buildings along Douglas Street [Yale's Chinatown], some of them in very poor circumstances."[40] There was also a story about desperate workers scrambling for frozen potatoes thrown out on Yale's Front Street.[41]

By the time Donald A. Smith, a major CPR stockholder and director whose influence had proven so crucial, drove the railroad's final spike at Craigellachie, B.C., on November 7,

1885, most of the 2,900 Chinese had already drifted out of the construction camps toward the west coast, the United States, or eastward toward the Maritimes in search of work. There were also doctors, barbers, vegetable sellers, butchers, wood cutters and cafe owners who had provided services to the railway workers and who had to move now that the construction sites were dismantled. Some of these immigrants settled in the small towns along the rail line instead of heading for the west coast or out of B.C. Doctors set up practices in places like Soda Dog Creek, the Lillooet district and Yale. Merchants established themselves in every village and town along the line, and miners found work in Hope, Cassiar, Lytton, Lillooet, Dog Creek and as far north as the Cariboo and Quesnel Forks.[42]

Most of the Chinese who moved west eventually reached Victoria, still the best source of work because it possessed the oldest and most firmly-established Chinatown in Canada. As well, Victoria remained the most important seaport linking China and Canada. While Vancouver would eventually outstrip it in population and influence during the 1930s, Victoria was still the clearing point for all Chinese travellers leaving or returning to Canada, Seattle or Portland.

Those rail hands who headed east passed through the Rockies to Lethbridge and on to Calgary, Edmonton, Medicine Hat or Saskatchewan. Some in Alberta found work as miners, but most took up the only jobs left to them: in laundries and cafes. A few became grocers, bunkhouse cooks, market gardeners and servants to the white elite.

In self-defence, the Chinese in Alberta, as in other provinces, congregated in Chinatowns. By the turn of the century, Calgary had Alberta's largest Chinatown. Because of urban expansion and the inability of the Chinese to buy any land outright, Calgary's Chinatown was forced to move twice between 1900 and 1910. By 1911, its population leveled off at 1,700.[43]

If the racism of white Albertans, or simple bad luck, persuaded Chinese immigrants to move on to Swift Current,

Saskatchewan, along the rail line, they would find a tiny speck of a community which by January, 1923, had a total of 23 bachelors operating laundries and restaurants, one woman who was a maid to the only Chinese merchant in town, and two teenage boys. One of them, Deep Quong, was among the last Chinese immigrants to arrive in Canada before the exclusion act of 1923. The son of a Chinese official in the Qing government who moved to Toronto after World War II, he probably also caught a glimpse of Moose Jaw on his way to Swift Current. By 1911 a growing Chinese community of 160 people and 20 businesses made Moose Jaw the largest Chinese community and in Saskatchewan; Regina, Saskatoon and Battleford also had Chinatowns of their own.[44]

Leaving Saskatchewan, a traveller passed through Brandon, with its small Chinese community, to Winnipeg, where old-timers would tell of their city's first Chinese, who arrived in the late 1850s. (The Winnipeg *Free Press*, however, reported that on November 18, 1877, four workers who came to Manitoba by stagecoach from the United States were that city's first Chinese.) By the time of the exclusion act, Winnipeg's Chinese population consisted of more than 790 bachelors and 22 women. The surnames of Lee, Wong and Mah dominated; there were only four families in the entire city. Many came from the Guangdong provincial districts of Haoshan, Taishan, Nanhai, Panyu and Shunde.[45]

Leaving Manitoba for Toronto, Chinese itinerants passed through small patches of Chinese communities in Kenora, Port Arthur (now Thunder Bay), Sudbury and finally into Toronto, the capital city of Ontario. In contrast to Victoria's close community of 3,280 in 1884, a traveller found Toronto's population of 100 Chinese laborers and merchants scattered throughout the city. Some immigrants were said to have arrived as early as 1877 or 1878; in 1881, 10 Chinese settled in Toronto, and were soon followed by about 90 more after work on the CPR ended.

By 1900, a Chinatown was forming between Parliament and Yonge along Queen Street. Since it was located close to the business heart of the city, Toronto developed in and around Chinatown. In 1911, 228 businesses, mostly laundries, employed many of the 1,031 Chinese settlers in a Toronto which now had a population of 130,000. Four years later, Chinatown expanded westward toward Bay Street and the old city hall, where a large market community was located. Cafe owners, launderers, grocers, barbers and market gardeners were able to stabilize their businesses in this area, which formed the hub of the Chinese community until 1936, when Chinatown moved again. By the late 1920s, Chinatown was a community of a little over 2,000 people, working, raising families, exercising in athletic associations, acting in dramatic societies and betting in the merchant-run gambling halls.[46]

Southwest of Toronto, Chinese communities sprang up in Hamilton, London and Windsor. Of the three, Hamilton was the most important because of its proximity to Toronto. The first immigrant reached the city, probably from Toronto, in 1880 or 1881. By 1901, an energetic community was developing in the city centre, near city hall, the market area, the train station and the main highway heading toward Toronto. Despite the economic depression then affecting Hamilton, the Chinese community was able to develop a firm and stable base. The community's leadership was assumed by merchants such as Fong Young, who at 26 moved from Ottawa and established Hamilton's first Chinese-owned restaurant, and John G. Lee, a laundry owner who was the president of a marriage bureau for bachelors called the Chinese Women's Organization. The marriage bureau was especially important for the growth of Chinatown because its main objective was to establish settled families in Hamilton, thus helping to eliminate the myth of the transient associated with the bachelor life.

Hamilton's Chinatown grew steadily until 1910, the year the city's aldermen passed two by-laws aimed at preventing its further growth. By-law 73 prohibited the setting up of laundries in areas where such businesses already existed. This prevented the establishment of new laundries in Chinatown, where the laundries' clientele lived, and where it was least expensive to set up a business. Operating costs in other neighborhoods were prohibitively higher, and business would be slower. The effect of by-law 73 was to halt the growth of business in Chinatown.

The other anti-Chinese regulation, by-law 74, prohibited a laundry from using its premises for lodging or for gambling. Travellers and newly-arrived Chinatown residents were frequently put up in laundries for short periods of time; additionally, it was well known to Hamilton's police that laundries also served as leisure time recreation areas for the community's bachelor workers. This second by-law thus attempted to control the activities of the Chinese, and together with the first, destroyed Chinatown as a compact community. A traveller arriving in Hamilton in 1920 would find a declining Chinese community scattered throughout the city.[47]

Continuing eastward, the next large Chinatown would be found in Montreal. On the way, a traveller could stop off at small Chinese settlements in Kingston and Ottawa, whose Chinese population in 1902 was 100. In 1880, the Montreal *Star* reported that the city's Chinese community was 30 residents, working in laundries and other businesses. By 1921, there were about 600 businesses and 1,603 Chinese settlers in Montreal.

In Quebec City could be found another small Chinese community of 60 bachelor workers living around Cote d'Abraham in 1910 and later on east St. Vallier. In 1911, the community absorbed 50 Chinese newcomers. By 1940, the Chinese population reached 230, with 50 working in laundries and the rest in restaurants. But Quebec City's Chinese community grew slowly because, like Edmonton and Saskatoon, it did not lie along the CPR's route.[48]

Those who ventured east past Montreal found only sparse Chinese settlements in the Atlantic provinces. By the 1930s, only about 300 Chinese made their homes in New Brunswick, with the majority living in Fredericton.[49] In Nova Scotia and Newfoundland, the Chinese settlements revolved around the family of entrepreneur Fong Choy. Leaving his village in

Enping district of Guangdong province, Fong set out for England in the 1880s. From Europe, he managed the Atlantic crossing and settled in Montreal, the port of entry on the east coast. Later he moved to Halifax, where he and a relative opened a laundry in 1895. In time, immigrants with surnames other than Fong began arriving in Halifax by way of Victoria, Toronto and Montreal. By 1916, about 100 bachelors lived in Halifax, most running laundries and restaurants. Three years later, the wife of a laundry owner named Lee joined her husband and son, Chuck, and the Lees became the first Chinese family in Nova Scotia's capital.[50]

Fong Choy also had a hand in building the Chinese community in Newfoundland. In the same year that he opened a laundry in Halifax (which he later sold), Fong set up a laundry with a partner named Wang Chang in St. John's. They announced that "Sing Lee & Co. Chinese laundries will be ready to receive work on Monday at their laundry, 37 New Gower Street, corner Holdsworth Street." The notice, printed in local newspapers, was dated August 24, 1895.

By 1904, the Lee Wah Laundry at 239 New Gower Street and the Kam Lung Laundry at 11 Cochrane Street began to rival the Sing Lee & Co. for business. But work was still plentiful until 1906, the year the Newfoundland house of assembly created a head tax of $300 for all new Chinese settlers. At this time, the population of the Chinese community stabilized between 120 and 130.[51]

Some of the more fortunate ex-rail hands moved to Victoria in search of work and human company. Once there they headed straight for Chinatown, which took in four blocks around Fisgard Street. By 1884, they would have found other Chinese workers in many occupations. While Victoria alone had 130 Chinese bootmakers, the most common jobs were in the laundries, restaurants and domestic service. But in British Columbia as a whole, the Chinese found work in many other areas. In 1884, 7,200 of the entire Chinese adult male population of 9,870 was employed on the railways and farms and in mining, mills and canning. The other 2,670 were working as cooks, domestics, merchants, store employees and in laundries. In addition, there were the self-employed who provided services in Chinatown as barbers, doctors, butchers and other occupations.[52]

In 1902, Victoria's Chinatown was still located within the city limits. Its population had levelled off at 3,280 (less during the canning season). It was able to serve all the common laborer's needs.

# BACHELOR SOCIETY

"Bachelor" workers, many with wives and children to support in China, economized in every aspect of life in Canada. Many of the cooks, laundry employees and domestic laborers, earning from $20 to $30 a month, lived in crowded boarding houses because this was all they could afford. A typical building used to lodge Chinese workers in Victoria was three stories high with a floor space of 10 by 30 feet. Some rooms with ten-foot ceilings were partitioned into two—not side-by-side but up-and-down! Twice the rent was exacted by making two storeys out of one.

The lower floor was split into small rooms separated from the outer walls by hallways so narrow, two adults could barely squeeze by one another. Each room had three low bunks covered by a mat and one or two quilts. While the second floor was a replica of the first, the third floor was even gloomier, and lacking any source of fresh air and being lit only by a kerosene lamp.

Unable to afford even these lodgings, workers earning less than $20 a month had to settle for single-storey boarding houses. Constructed of rough timber and closely resembling lumber or railroad camp bunkhouses, these primitive accommodations were a common sight in the heart of Victoria's Chinatown. Inside, workers shared a ten-foot-square room with five others in a double tier of three bunks, each bed covered with a mat. With only one small pane of glass, sunlight and ventilation were at a premium.

The Vancouver housing situation was also bleak. In one two-storey Chinatown rooming house known as the Armstrong, 27 rooms, each twenty feet long and thirteen feet wide with ten-foot ceilings, were sectioned off on the second floor. Each room contained a square table, six beds, and a single stove, on which the men cooked rice, preserved duck, eggs and vegetables. Each worker paid 50 cents a month in rent. On Carrall Street, another lodging house had 19 rooms for 50 laborers at $2.50 to $3 a month.[1]

### Poppies

Forced to return from their low-paying jobs to crowded, dismal, unsanitary rooming houses, many lonely and despondent laborers turned to opium as an alternative to madness. Ever since British merchants, backed by Her Majesty's gunboats, realized that vast profits could be made by selling opium in China's huge market of 400 million, the drug was easily available in any country touched by Britain's special brand of imperialism.

Opium came into Canada during the nineteenth century from the British colony of Hong Kong and the United States. After a slow start, the import value of the Hong Kong variety exploded from $810 in the initial year of business in 1862 to $6,640 the following year. From then on, imports increased steadily. In 1880, Canada became the only legal outlet of opium in North America when the United States government passed a law prohibiting the production and sale of opium.[2] (That was a prelude to its own exclusion act, passed in 1882.) Since Chinese involvement in the opium trade was a matter of

75

fact in the eyes of the law makers, the act was directed against the Chinese community.

By 1880, 372,880 pounds of opium had passed through San Francisco to British Columbia. The American ban on opium forced drug merchants to move their factories to Victoria's Chinatown. By 1883, the city's eleven opium shops, with an annual take of over $3 million, had become the main North American producers and distributors of this reddish-brown, heavily-scented drug. The trade was so lucrative that even the British Columbia government took its cut by imposing a $500 yearly license fee.[3]

Most of the drug was transported by CPR employees from Asia to Canada's west coast and then on to Toronto and Montreal. In contrast to the strict controls on liquor, drugs received little attention from lawmakers. In the 1880s and 1890s, opium affected few white Canadians and therefore was not considered a social problem; that it ruined the lives of Chinese immigrants was of little consequence. However, the police did seize shipments which appeared to be destined for the United States. In 1891, a consignment of 141 pounds was confiscated in Swift Current. A saloon in Sweet Grass, Montana, was shut down when the Northwest Mounted Police told their American counterparts that it was a transfer point for opium entering the United States. But while Canadian police were often indifferent to users of the drug, surveillance of known drug traffickers was another matter. One of these smugglers was Donald McLean, better known as "Little Dan" or "Opium Dan," who worked on a Pacific steamer while selling drugs. Police speculated that Mclean's activities netted him at least $15,000.[4]

While there were countless small-time operators like Opium Dan, a few Chinese merchants extracted a fortune from the drug trade, capitalizing on the loneliness of Chinese workers in North America. From the time of the gold rush days in California and British Columbia until well after the railways were finished, 40 to 50 per cent of the Chinese were addicted to the drug, which cost 80 cents for a little more than an ounce. In the late 1880s, the cost soared to $1.20. By 1901, three Victoria firms with eighteen partners had established a monopoly in the manufacture of opium. Seven years later, opium production was outlawed by the Canadian government. Driving the trade underground caused prices to skyrocket.[5]

By the time opium had been made illegal, many Chinese (and whites) were already addicts. Chinese associations typically had the drug on hand at all their meetings. But the bulk of the opium eaters or smokers were the bachelor workers, who would drown their sorrows in the drug. Opium houses, like taverns and saloons, were accessible and stocked with an assortment of brands and the latest paraphernalia.

Opium smokers used a pipe about the length and thickness of a flute. The tip of the pipe was flattened to accommodate the smoker's lips. At the other end of the stem was a terra cotta bowl about the size of a *demi tasse*. The opium, dark gummy paste, was rolled into a pea-sized ball, placed in the bowl of the pipe, and lit. The average addict needed about twelve pipefuls at a sitting to achieve the full effect.[6]

### Fantan Alley

Gambling parlors owned and operated by Chinese merchants were open night and day to bachelor workers with time to kill after a shift cleaning house at a white minister's home or ironing shirts for a local judge. From the days of the gold rush in 1858, gambling had been an important part of Chinatown life. Leisure moments away from the sand bars and, later, the railroads, were spent at games of chance. Hustlers, working on ocean freighters, ferries and railways, with quick hands and an instinct for the weakness of others, set the stakes and rules. For the Chinese laborer without a woman or family, the wandering dealer provided a necessary service. In time, colorful tales and a romantic aura sprang up around these adventurers. Stories of their deeds and travels to exotic places excited the imagination of many young men who found Chinatown confining and dull. Repetitious work in a laundry or restaurant fueled their longing for excitement, and the intinerant gambler became a romantic hero. His lifestyle was especially seductive to young people who might be growing up in the back of a shop and being inculcated in the Confucian values of respecting one's elders and maintaining the social harmony of status-conscious and conservative Chinatown. A merchant's son was better off leaving behind his fantasies of leading the life of the gambler; sons were a precious resource in the early Chinese communities, and conformity and obedience were drilled into them so they might provide continuity and stability. The socialization process was generally effective, laying a foundation for the continuity of business and family in the Chinese community.

The itinerant gambler's unstable, transient lifestyle was at odds with the development of a Chinese community, which needed stability to survive and flourish in a hostile environment. But his presence on the frontier of Chinese Canada was not designed to benefit a staid, family-oriented society; he was like a travelling medicine show entertaining the lonely laborer and bringing news of China and Chinatown. The professional Chinese gambler catered to the scattered Chinese, moving from one wilderness camp or ship to another. The Chinatowns, too, were dotted with gambling houses, established by the merchant pillars of the Chinese community. The first organized betting activity started in Victoria's Fantan Alley, famous in Chinese communities throughout North America as "Bank Street." At its peak, after the completion of the CPR in 1884, Fantan Alley had twelve houses of chance as well as several restaurants catering to hungry gamblers.

Not more than 200 feet long and so narrow that two people could not pass without brushing, Fantan Alley was little more than a corridor. Constantly crowded with a variety of people, the alley was not only the hot spot for gambling but also a place for conducting business or just meeting friends.

A hundred bettors could jam into the various booths of a large gambling establishment while the smaller places accommodated several dozen gamblers. Inside a gambling house, high-rolling hustlers and pimps sporting the latest San Francisco styles were elbow to elbow with simple laborers in their cotton garments, and paunchy merchants wearing fine suits. Outside, the air was thick with the solicitations of hawkers of prepared meals, ready-made clothing, high-tone boots, potent brews or whatever else a customer might want, but inside the booths was a tomb-like silence, broken only by the occasional clicking of cash pieces or bamboo tiles.

In Fantan Alley's heyday, women singers, acrobats and even Chinese opera players were brought from San Francisco to entertain in the gambling houses or in a merchant-owned theatre. Opera tickets, at 5 to 20 cents, were within the means of even the poorest laborers.[7] Such diversions, however, could not compete with the serious business of trying to get something for nothing. Laborers might lose a day's pay in an hour of betting, and restaurants and laundries could change hands in the course of an evening. Games like *paijiu*, sparrow, *paiju*, dominoes, *tianjiu*, policy, mahjong and fantan could relieve even the most experienced player of his life savings, or increase a worker's already burdensome obligations to his immigration broker.

The most popular game was policy, a lottery or numbers game. Since the initial bet could be as low as a nickel or a dime and the payoff was potentially enormous, a worker could play for hours until his penny-ante stash dried up. In its simplest form, a player would bet 5 cents, for example, on the total paid attendance at a theatre showing a Chinese opera on a particular day. The odds meant there were many losers, but a player who correctly guessed the number could win $25 on a 25 cent bet at odds of 100 to one—a considerable payoff in those days.[8]

For the high rollers, the big game was fantan. The betting could vary from a dime to hundreds of dollars, and fantan, unlike policy, involved some skill. Holding a tapered whalebone stick carved to a small bow, the dealer sat at the front of a rectangular table with an inverted tin bowl by his elbow. After calling for the players to place their bets (by tossing in a traditional round cash piece made of brass and

79

characterized by a square hole in the centre), the dealer would close the bets suddenly and rake in the pieces with the whalebone stick. They were counted, except for the last handful, which were concealed. Bets were then taken on the number of pieces left and whether the number was odd or even.[9]

Although gambling was a popular way of passing leisure hours, the players usually left the gaming tables empty-handed. The house rule was winner take all, and the merchants who ran the houses amassed a fortune.

### Blaming the Victim

Another enterprise that filled the coffers of some merchants was prostitution. As well as establishing branch businesses to sell confectionary goods, clothing, rice and other necessary items in Victoria and Vancouver, San Francisco entrepreneurs exported girls and young women specifically groomed for prostitution to Canada's early Chinatowns. Soon after the movement of miners and laborers through Victoria to the sandbars of the Fraser River, brothels were set up in the cities and towns along the mining trails.

While white prostitution in Victoria outnumbered Chinese prostitutes 150 to 4 in 1902,[10] the presence of Chinese prostitutes once again symbolized a separation of the races, even in the most intimate of matters. Mixing of the races was a taboo unless it involved white men and Chinese women. In 1922, Emily F. Murphy, the first woman judge in the British empire, called "sexual relations between white women and Chinese men the ultimate in human degradation." The judge went on to observe that "in marital relations between white women and men of color, the glove is always thrown by the woman, or, at least deliberately dropped."[11] In popular literature, however, it was the Chinese men who were accused of "violating" white women. The *Canadian Magazine* alleged that Chinese men in Toronto chased white women because the head tax prevented Chinese wives and families from joining their men. Toronto's *Jack Canuck* magazine's readers learned that "yellow friends" were demoralizing "our young womanhood" by luring them into sin with opium.[12] These attitudes symbolized a whole century of white Canadian attitudes toward miscegenation between Chinese and whites.

Some Chinese merchants quickly realized that profits could be made from the sexual needs of Chinese workers and the curiosity of white pleasure seekers. The first prostitutes were brought from the flesh market in San Francisco, the centre of the slave trade for Asian women. Reflecting the class differences between merchants and laborers, the brothels were divided between the higher-status and better-paying parlor work, and the less-esteemed crib prostitution.

Women working in the parlors took the higher-paying merchants and white customers into comfortable, opulent entertainment rooms. Crib prostitutes were forced to depend on their wage-earning customers to keep their pimps in the latest fashions, and themselves alive. The "cribs," each of which held up to six women, were slatted crates, often located out of doors, measuring approximately 12 feet by 14 feet with a curtain, pallet, wash basin, mirror and usually two chairs. A woman forced into crib prostitution would work for six to eight years; at the end of her usefulness, when she was ravaged by disease, physical abuse or starvation, she was allowed to escape to the Salvation Army, the hospital or the gutter. Typically, she would be dead within six months.[13]

The sale of Chinese women in San Francisco, while illegal, was in fact widely known and condoned. The San Francisco *Chronicle* reported that "the particularly fine portions of the cargo, the fresh and pretty females who came from the interior, are used to fill special orders from wealthy merchants and prosperous tradesmen." Merchants from Victoria were part of the audience that saw women "stripped and paraded onto a platform where prospective buyers could inspect and bid."[14]

These Chinese women were bought and sold as commodities in a market that raised their price from a low of $500 to a high of $2,500 after the United States exclusion act of 1882.[15] By

1886, when workers from the railway camps surged west, women and young girls from poverty-stricken peasant and workers' families in Guangdong, Jiangsi and Zhejiang provinces were arriving in Victoria and Vancouver direct from overseas. The most coveted prostitutes were children, ranging from six years old to the late teens.[16]

In rural China, the feudal outlook regarded female children to be inferior to their brothers. Women were thought unable to provide the muscle power necessary for farm work, and the birth of a girl in a peasant family was cause for sorrow. Within the Confucian value system based on male supremacy, women were expendable from the day of their birth. A father who had only daughters could at best hope for a prosperous son-in-law, requests for a concubine from a wrinkled but wealthy merchant, official, or well-off peasant, or an order from a gentry for bondmaids. Women in feudal China served no useful purpose except as sexual objects, baby makers or beasts of burden. If none of these options materialized and times were severe, especially during or after civil wars or rebellions, a father sought out a brothel-keeper to try to interest him in his most attractive daughters. Custom and economic crisis forced Chinese families to look down on their daughters. The selling of female children and young women into the flesh market was the last desperate attempt to keep the remaining members of the family together.

The inequality and brutal use of women was nothing new in China. Prostitution in North America was simply the New World version of this exploitation. No one in the Chinese community tried to stop the trade in human cargo, except the occasional love-sick bachelor. But romantic efforts to rescue a woman from her preordained degradation led inevitably to a beating of the would-be knight, administered by the woman's pimps. These enforcers provided the muscle that kept the coffers of a few merchants filled. They also blocked white evangelists in their efforts to save the souls of these "depraved" Chinese women.

These women, victims of a misogynist society in China and

slaves to a handful of rich merchants in North America, fell easy prey to the evangelism of white missionaries in the New World. The lure of the kingdom of heaven was strong for someone who likely faced syphilitic death before the age of 25. The most famous rescue centre for victims of the prostitution business was Miss Morgan's Chinese Girls' Home in Victoria. Established in 1888 and supported by the Women's Missionary Society of the Methodist Church, the home specialized in helping Chinese girls and women escape the clutches of the pimps and their bosses. No one was forced to take refuge in the home; as Miss Morgan said, "Unless they want us to help them, we can't help them."[17] Saving the souls of Chinese prostitutes became the "white woman's burden."[18]

Between 1888 and 1902, the home rescued from prostitution 40 Chinese and 8 Japanese girls and women between the ages of 7 and 24. Twenty-two married Chinese laborers, 4 remained at Miss Morgan's, 3 returned to their old life, and the rest returned to China. All were baptised and brought into the Methodist faith. Those who were forced back into prostitution provoked Miss Morgan and her staff into legal action. On one occasion, it cost $120 in legal fees to reclaim a runaway; on another, $270.

When the Chinese Girls' Home became a well-known rescue centre, many laborers began to frequent the place, ostensibly interested in Christianity. But, said Miss Morgan, a Chinese bachelor "will profess to become a Christian to get a wife."

There were other refuges like Miss Morgan's which tried to help runaways. But there were also those who tried to profit from the misery of these women. In one case, an individual by the name of Mains enticed young women into his home, offering protection from the pimps and the hope of a new life. There was, however, nothing new in the life he offered; Mains was eventually sentenced to 8 months of hard labor for the abduction and sale of women for prostitution.[19]

That prostitution was an economic transaction among men rather than the result of a woman's depravity was emphasized by Lee Mon-kow, a Chinese interpreter at the customs house in

Victoria. A resident of the city since 1882, Lee told the 1902 Royal Commission on Chinese and Japanese Immigration that a contract was usually drawn up between a brothel dealer and a Chinese merchant who agreed to pay the woman's head tax, passage costs and expenses. In return, the contractor "had the right to her body service." She undertook "to pay a certain sum at a certain time, to repay the passage money and the head tax and seven per cent interest." In one case cited by Lee, a woman named Woon Ho cost a merchant $302 plus $7 for clothing and $4 for her leather trunk.[20]

Despite the low ratio of Chinese prostitutes to white prostitutes, a handful of Chinese merchants in the flesh trade made large profits catering to both Chinese and white men. Their control over Chinese prostitution, combined with their stranglehold on opium, gambling and immigration brokerage, gave these entrepreneurs immense power over the destinies of bachelor workers.

### Welcome to Canada

One of the very few times when the merchants' long arm failed to touch bachelor workers was upon their first entrance into Victoria's Richet Wharf. Since Canada did not have immigration offices in Hong Kong or China, an immigration office especially for Asians was set up in Victoria. The last building used as a "detention hospital" was built in 1908 on the corner of Ontario and Dalls Streets. Here Chinese passengers were questioned, stripped, examined and told to pay the head tax. One Chinese immigrant's poem described the anguish of its author:

Fellow countrymen, read the following notice
  quickly:
Having amassed several hundred dollars,
I left my native home for a foreign land.
To my surprise, I was kept inside a prison cell!
Alas, there is nowhere for me to go from here,

I can neither see the world outside nor my dear
  parents.
When I think of this, my tears begin to stream
  down.
To whom can I confide my sorrow,
But to write a few lines in this room.[21]

This was the reception and reaction of many bachelor
workers. By the time they left the "prison walls" of the
Canadian government, they quickly fell under the influence of
the merchant class and its life style. In many ways, the Chinese
merchant world was an attempt to transplant the values and
customs of a country across the Pacific.

# Banding Together

In 1885, the ex-rail hands, merchants and other Chinese arriving in Victoria would have marvelled at the many developments in their community. The most important was the establishment of the Chinese Consolidated Benevolent Association in 1884. Located at 558 Fisgard Street in an old joss house, the CBA opened its doors to any Chinese travelling through or living in Victoria. For the first time in Canadian history there was a merchant association helping Chinese immigrants in need. The CBA's founders, in a February, 1884, letter to Huang Cunxian, the Qing dynasty consul-general in San Francisco, seeking his help in setting up a Chinese Canadian association, stated three reasons for establishing such an organization. Their greatest fear was the spread of racism from American agitators whose presence in Canada would provoke higher head taxes and additional legislation aimed at preventing Chinese immigration. Second, they feared laws excluding Chinese people already in Canada from certain jobs and from living in certain areas; a central body dedicated to fighting for the rights of the Chinese people in Canada was a necessity. Finally, the organizers were concerned about "a few who have joined local Westerners in bullying their own fellow Chinese." They also found that prostitution and gambling was prevalent, giving rise to increased bickering and street fights within the Chinese community. A CBA was a necessity if racist Canadian laws were to be opposed, Chinese prostitution eliminated and the Chinese people in Canada united.[1]

Taking on the social welfare functions which had been a gentry-merchant tradition in China, the CBA looked after the sick, penniless, homesick worker. After the completion of the CPR, jobless laborers who were able to catch the sympathetic ear of the CBA's president, Lee Yau-kum (Li Youqin) or secretary Chu Wai-san (Xu Weisan), could find themselves with a one-way ticket back to China. However, the CBA's constitution stipulated that only the unemployed over 60 were eligible for this free trip home, and few were able to take advantage of the association's generosity.

The association also cared for the sick, but not for free; all expenses had to be repaid once health was regained. Funeral services were also provided, but only to those without relatives in Canada. At other times, lodging was secured for the homeless.

The association's services existed, in part, to tell the public that there was a permanent and stable institution dedicated to the aid of the Chinese people in Canada, that problems affecting the Chinese would be taken care of by the Chinese people themselves. But while relief assistance was part of its function, the CBA's major objectives were more complex.[2]

During the construction of Onderdonk's section of the railway, 15,000 Chinese immigrants arrived in Canada. Such a large body of laborers travelling through British Columbia naturally sparked human conflicts. Disputes over property, rowdiness, cheating on gambling tables, and countless other difficulties required an arbiter of social harmony and political stability, so necessary if the prosperity of merchant business was to prevail. By 1884, there were Chinese communities of various sizes in 30 cities and towns scattered throughout British

Columbia, and an ombudsman was needed to adjudicate everything from minor quarrels to shoot-outs. By this time, the merchant pillars of Chinese society were sufficiently secure to establish a permanent "court," policing agency and welfare bureau in one association. After some years of negotiations and compromise, 31 local groups in Victoria came together to establish the CBA as an umbrella organization. Its by-laws stated that the association would "arbitrate in monetary disputes between Chinese if the parties involved come to ask the Association's mediation." Potentially the organization held wide powers within the community. Another by-law suggested an access to powers greater than itself. "If a Chinese gangster has a grudge against the Association's directors and avenges himself on them, the Association will report him to the Chinese Consul-General, the British authorities and the local authority in China, so that he will be arrested for trial." Other articles concerned white Canadians. "If a Westerner assaults, robs or refuses to pay his debts to a Chinese, and if he makes a complaint to the Association, the Association will assist him to appeal to the law." In another, "if a Chinese is wrongly accused by a Westerner and jailed, the Association will obtain bail for him and employ a lawyer to appeal against the sentence."[3]

The CBA also fought the efforts of racists who called for legislation to increase the notorious head taxes. Almost from its inception in 1884, the CBA collected $2 from every Chinese resident to create a defence fund against any future attempts by the larger Canadian society to institutionalize racism.[4]

Because of its well-connected membership, the CBA was able to facilitate the collection of the $2 as well as broaden its influence. Organizations affiliated with the CBA touched almost every Chinese person through kinship, business, political, religious and social affiliations. They included district benevolent associations such as the Toishan (Taishan) & Ning yeung (Ningyang), Hoiping (Kaiping) and Chungshan (Zhongshan). There were also the Kwangchow (Guangzhou), Hoiping (Kaiping) and Yan Ping (Yanping) associations. A dialect organization called the Sun Yup (Sanyi) Natives

Association was also affiliated, as were groups representing such surnames as Lee (Li), Wong (Wang), Mah (Ma), Lam (Lin) and Chan (Chen). There were also the Oi Lin (Ai Lian) or Love Lotus Association, Ng Shei Shan (Wu Shishan) Hall, Tit sheng shung yi wai (Tiehchang Xiongyi), or Respect Justice Association, Chinese Chamber of Commerce (Zhonghua shanghui), Tung yun (Tongyuan) Association, Chinese Nationalist Party (Zhongguo guomin dang), Hongmen Minchi Party, United Church Association, Hua Sheng Athletic Society, United Youth Association, Chinese Prodice Association, Chinese Young Christian Association, Tat Kun (Dakun) Society, Han Yun (Hanyuan) or Leisure Garden Club, and Lock Yun (Leyuan) or Pleasant Garden Club.[5]

The CBA was essential for the survival of the Chinese people in Canada. Without it destitute Chinese laborers had nowhere to turn for help; the sick would be left to die, corpses unattended to, lawlessness would have been the norm, and racists would be unopposed. Further immigration would have remained unorganized and subject to even greater abuse. The establishment of the CBA was a real attempt to remedy these problems. Although it was unsuccessful against the head taxes, the CBA was the first national body in Canada set up by the Chinese people to fight racial discrimination.

Before the CBA existed to represent Chinese Canadian interests, communication between Chinese leaders in Canada and government officials at all levels had to take a time-consuming and bureaucratically awkward route through the office of the consul-general in San Francisco. The CBA also provided the mechanism and infrastructure for merchant control of the Chinese community in Canada (and the evolution of a distinct life style founded on the values and customs of a commercial class). By taking over the functions of the consul-general, the CBA became a *de facto* Chinese government in Canada.

## Feudalism in Gold Mountain

The CBA's relationship with Chinese workers resembled the feudal relationship between the gentry-patron class and the peasantry in China. Paternalistic in spirit, the association adopted the social obligations which wealthier, usually elder members of the Chinese community in Canada believed to be their responsibility, i.e., to provide social welfare assistance to the less fortunate.

Before the 1911 revolution that toppled the Qing dynasty, the gentry, by virtue of its superior education and its social status as part of the scholar class, was obliged to perform many functions, including local registration and police work, providing educational programs for the peasantry, overseeing sanitation and public works, and setting up relief for the destitute. It was the role and duty of the elite class in China to help the less fortunate and poorer classes. This was especially true when members of the gentry could not secure government positions. In order to help the state maintain social control, these individuals would perform these local services. Conservative in perspective, the gentry was the watch dog and defender of the status quo in dynastic China.[6] In many ways, the gentry followed the dictum of the Song (960-1279) dynasty official Fu Bi, who warned that "when desperate characters study and attend examinations but find no hope of success, they often grow disgruntled, develop rebellious ideas, and secretly conspire with one another. These types are scattered among the people and can really cause disasters. Thus it is important to gain their confidence and thereby bridle them."[7]

The CBA's purpose was not to support the status quo of the white world, but to establish a hierarchy in the Chinese community with merchants and entrepreneurs occupying the top rungs. The association was planting stable roots in Canada, creating a well-defined social structure of two classes, merchants and laborers, and providing the foundation for an organized community life. In many ways, the establishment of the CBA, its organizational roots and structure, and its Canadian-influenced policies clearly demonstrated that the

Chinese were determined to become part of Canada. "Desperate characters" in the Chinese community therefore had to be bridled so the developing merchant class could grow and prosper. Maintaining local community control by deflecting potential rebellion among the working class helped to prevent the white world from intervening and perhaps destroying the foundations of a fledgling Chinese community. It was, of course, also a way of enhancing a merchant life style.

### Secret Society

Another Chinese organization, made up of smaller merchants and workers, was founded as a clandestine brotherhood association in 1862 in the gold mining city of Barkerville, B.C. The Chikongtang (Zhigongtang), also known as the Hongmen (Chinese Freemasons), was a branch of the anti-Qing dynasty secret society called the Triads. Like the CBA, the Chikongtang provided social welfare assistance to the predominantly bachelor workers who labored in the mines on the west coast and in the Cariboo area. The recipients of aid usually had no kinship ties in Canada.[8]

The Chikongtang, however, was not principally concerned with its Canadian activities. Its main goal was the overthrow of the Qing government in China. Social aid programs in Canada were important tools for gathering overseas recruits, spreading anti-Qing propaganda and raising money for the struggle in China. Its avowed revolutionary aims made the Chikongtang and its parent organization in China, the Triads, outlaw organizations.[9] In China, the penalty for membership was death.

Their seditious activities were wrapped in veils of ritual and secrecy. Among the 36 sworn oaths was the promise "not to debauch a brother's wife, daughter, or sister: if you do, may you perish under the knife." Members pledged "not [to] avenge private animosity under the pretext of a public wrong, thus covertly scheming to injure a brother: if you do, may you be bitten by a tiger when you ascend a hill, may you drown when you go into water."[10]

Certain intricate mannerisms and signs were used to detect the true member and to ferret out government spies. At mealtimes "stretch your fingers and place the chop sticks across them, and offer them to a stranger, who, if a member, will then push the cup away from him." In a dark alley, a society member meeting another person will clench and raise a fist with the thumb pointing upward. If the other is also a member, a smile will immediately appear and apologies will follow.

Slang and secret code words were also important. The police were a "current of air"; to belong to a lodge was "to be born" (because "once entering the Hong doors, there is no kin, no history"); highway robbery was "shooting partridges"; looting a ship was "eating ducks"; and killing was "washing one's ears."[11]


## Setting Up Shop

Membership in the CBA, the Chikongtang or other Chinese organizations automatically opened up a wide assortment of contacts, privileges and opportunities. A bachelor looking for a wife could ask around in his local lodge or association chapter to assess the matrimonial market in Hong Kong, China or the Americas. Or, if the romantic aura of revolution struck a young man's fancy, the Chikongtang could always use an enthusiastic and loyal recruit, provided he came with the proper recommendations and introductions from veteran society members.

These association ties also provided support and money for anti-Qing revolutionaries like Sun Yat-sen, or Qing loyalist groups like the *Baohuanghui* (Protect the Emporer Society), led by the famous Confucian scholar Kang Youwei. Agents of both sides waged a relentless battle for the hearts and minds of the Chinese people in Gold Mountain.

For the young and ambitious, securing friendship in a powerful organization like the CBA was not only a social necessity, but also the first step toward building a profitable business. Cash was readily available to the entrepreneur or seasoned trader whose kinship or association ties opened the door to participation in a rotating credit association. Used in China for more than 800 years as a vehicle for raising money,[12] these financial organizations were easily adapted to accommodate Chinese communities. The credit system succeeded only to the extent that each member faithfully met his obligation of providing the necessary funds within the prescribed period. The credit associations relied on a trust that could develop and ripen only in long-standing friendship or kinship bonds.

The character of credit associations could vary widely. Some involved friendly dealings conducted over sumptuous meals. Others were no-nonsense business clubs based on straightforward cash bids. In the first case, ten friends or relatives would come together to raise money and to socialize. The organizer would establish monthly payment from each subscriber. Fifty dollars would be a typical amount. During the first month, then, the ten contributed a total of $500. In the next month, the organizer would buy a dinner costing $50 for the other ten and contribute his monthly $50 to the pot. A lottery would then be set up to determine the recipient of the second month's pot of $500. That person would be responsible for the next meal, again priced at $50. A lottery for the $500 would again be held, and the process would continue until every subscriber had received $500 and had partaken in ten banquets, all for a total cost of only $550.

In investment credit clubs where profits were the objective, vast sums were often subscribed. The organizer would ask for bids from usually a dozen investors who would pay $500 a month each. Instead of a lottery, secret bids would be tendered by each subscriber, consisting of an interest rate they would be willing to pay for a year's use of the pot—$6,000 in this example. The money would go to the bidder offering the best rate of return, at the interest rate he bid. The return would be equally divided among the eleven unsuccessful bidders. An individual in need of a quick source of revenue thus would have to bid high to secure the monthly pot. As the need for the $6,000 gradually became less urgent for the remaining subscribers, the interest bids would drop. The bidder who remained without a pot throughout the first eleven months would in the final month submit a bid which was usually much lower than those of the others, who had already bid and taken their pot. Thus a shrewd merchant subscriber who could afford to wait until all the others had taken their turns borrowing money could pick up a tidy profit.[13]

The credit association was an ideal method by which to begin or expand a business. It was typically used for enterprises such as laundries, the most common of Chinatown businesses. The average laundry had ten workers including the owner. Small Victoria laundries run by men like Ming Lee, who opened for business in 1894, and Sun San-cheng, who had been in the trade for eighteen years in 1902, faced an average monthly overhead of $270, which included $7.20 for water, gas and electricity, $162 in wages for nine workers, $72 for their room and board, $10 for rent, $3.15 for insurance and $5.95 for city taxes. There was also a yearly $10 business fee.[14]

The minimum start-up capital required for one year was $3,240. Laborers who earned the going rate of $25 a month and saved $43 a year[15] after paying for the barest necessities would have had to work for 75 years before amassing the amount needed to set up a laundry business. The notion of many Westerners that the establishment of such a business needed limited capital, fueled by the appearance of so many of these "wash houses," was therefore false.[16] Yet Victoria did in 1902 have 40 Chinese laundries providing work for 197, Vancouver had 35 businesses employing 192, New Westminster had 9 shops and 38 workers, and Rossland had 20 staffed by 60 hired hands. Many small communities in British Columbia also had one or more laundry houses.[17]

Another trade that might interest an ambitious young entrepreneur was tailoring. One of the most successful was Charlie Bo, whose average monthly gross at the turn of the century was $900, derived from custom shirts and suits (standard or three-piece) at $12 to $20 per suit. His monthly production averaged 15 suits for whites plus 18 to 20 for Chinese customers. From the $900, Bo paid his six hired tailors $30 to $40 a month, and paid for materials, supplies and other sundries.[18]

As in the laundry business, the initial investment required for establishing a tailor shop was prohibitive for an individual laborer. While the credit clubs could be used to raise some capital, it was usually inadequate, and other sources were required. Often, the solution was to go into partnership. Almost all of the 109 Victoria firms in 1902 were partnership businesses, involving 288 investors.[19] One case in which a business began as a partnership and evolved into a prosperous sole proprietorship was the Panama Cafe, run by Chan Dun. He started out in 1900 as a silent partner in a grocery venture in partnership with his kinsman Chan Sui. But Chan Dun was convinced there was a need for a restaurant catering exclusively to working class whites, and between 1902 and 1910 he operated, each time in partnerships, a series of cafes in the vicinity of Broad and Johnson Streets in Victoria's Chinatown, bearing such names as the Montreal, the White and the Tourist. In 1910 he bought the Panama Cafe from a Japanese entrepreneur who sold out to become a fisherman. Later, the Panama Cafe moved to a remodelled theatre at 1407 Government Street, where it remained until a nearby department store that supplied most of its customers closed in 1967.[20]

## Canada Across the Pacific

In addition to these small commercial enterprises, Chinatown was home to wholesalers and retailers in the import-export trade between China, Hong Kong, San Francisco and Canada. Trade between Asia and what is now British Columbia began as early as 1780, when British traders established a Canton-North America trade in ginseng and sea otter pelts, docking at an outpost on Vancouver Island. In

1784, a shipload of lumber left the west coast for South China. In return, Western traders received silk, tea and chinaware from Hong Kong and Macao. In 1815, the Northwest Company sent natural resources and animal goods worth $101,155 to China.[21]

Between 1874 and 1884, Canadian imports from China totalled $1,369,779, and almost $412,000 was paid in import duties. From July 1, 1882, to August 1, 1884, the duty paid by Chinese trading houses escalated from 11.2 per cent, or $87,459, of a total revenue of $798,605 at the end of June, 1883, to 12.54 per cent, or $99,780, of $790,676 at the end of June, 1884, and finally to 25 per cent, or $19,320, of $77,208 in the month of July, 1884.

The main products entering Canada were rice, tea, liquors, tobacco, dry goods, chinaware, drugs and herbs, paper, books and stationery, matting clothing, cotton cloth shoes, opium, and joss papers and sticks. In 1884, 41 million pounds of rice, at a Canadian duty of 2.5 cents per pound, made its way into Canada's Chinatowns. At a retail price of $6 per 100 pounds, rice cost more than twice as much as wheat flour, which sold for $2.50 per 100 pounds.

Chinese merchants regularly acted as intermediaries between white wholesalers and Chinese customers in the buying and selling of cloth goods, woollens, linen, cloth caps, matches, papers, soaps, tobacco, cigars, sugar, flour, nails, tools, plates, horses, carriages, wagons, watches, ropes, lamps, fuels, coal, boots, stockings, furs, kerosene, candles, ironware, glass and crockery. About 90 per cent of the clothing worn by Chinese laborers and merchants was made in the United States.

In addition to the almost half a million dollars paid to the Canadian government in duties from 1874 to 1884, Chinese residents in Victoria paid a total of $34,706 between 1879 and 1883 for trade licenses, water rents, road taxes and real estate dues.[22]

In 1901 Victoria had 189 Chinese firms. Fourteen trading houses imported $107,595 in goods from China. Victoria's Chinese spent four times that amount—$464,369—on

Canadian, British and American products. Customs duties paid by Chinese businesses amounted to $148,377. One hundred and nine businesses representing a total investment of $573,500 rented premises from white landlords; their taxes, utilities, insurance, postage and rents totalled $57,158. Property owned by the other 80 Chinese merchants was worth $296,000. The value of all other Chinese-owned British Columbia businesses outside of Victoria that same year was $997,899.[23]

That Chinese merchants helped to enrich the treasury of the government and the prosperity of the country was obvious. They contributed to Canada's wealth through imports, duties, head taxes, municipal fees, land taxes, and goods bought from white merchants. The size and profitability of the trade between China and Canada, and the importance to the economy of Chinese merchants here, were factors that could not be ignored when legislators drafted laws governing Chinese immigration. In this light, Ottawa's infamous order in council 1272 (known as the Chinese Immigration Act, or the exclusion act) seems at first glance incongruous. Aside from being the only legislation in the country's history barring a specific people because of their race, the exclusion act had a class bias. It prevented virtually any Chinese worker from entering Canada, but not all Chinese were barred; the merchant class, in the broad sense, was exempted. Businessmen, diplomats and their entourages and families, Canadians of Chinese descent, and Chinese students registered in Canadian colleges or universities, were allowed in. In the final analysis, the profits of Canadian traders, sources of government revenue, and the vital trade connections between China and Canada were what dictated which class of people could move to Canada after 1923.

# Merchant Society

The development of Chinese commerce in Canada provided the economic foundation for the evolution of a unique family structure and life style. At the heart of this resilient family-oriented community were cultural and religious values taken from traditional China and the Christian West.

Canada's first Chinese settlers, the crew of John Meares, landed in 1788, but the children of their union with native women became in time less Chinese and more indigenous in culture and language. Before long, traces of any Chinese cultural lineage were wiped out. The first wholly Chinese family to plant roots in Canada was the Chong Lee household, arriving in 1860. From that time until 1923, a small but steady flow of Chinese families migrated to British Columbia Chinatowns, where it was possible to establish small businesses such as restaurants and laundries, and it was possible to make a go of these enterprises largely because of the unity and cohesiveness of the Chinese family unit. Families as large as ten or twelve were necessary to counteract municipal by-laws prohibiting the hiring of white help and the chance of injury or death by roving bands of racist hoods.

Chinatown's fate was intimately tied to the growth and prosperity of each family, which typically lived in the back of a shop or above a cafe. Stable families provided the stable context in which the exchange of goods could go on uninterrupted. Values conducive to such an environment were deeply rooted in Chinese culture. And while imperial and republican scholars spent their time after the Taiping Rebellion in 1864 debating the relevance of Confucianism and the applicability of Western technology to China, the Chinese in Gold Mountain held onto the Confucian ideas and values that accompanied them to the New World. In many ways, the hostile circumstances of their new homeland allowed them no alternative but to retain an attachment to their old world.

A humanist philosophy, Confucianism defined the proper order and status of human relationships. Founded by Kong Fuci (Master Kong) or Confucius (522-479 BC), it developed during the so-called Spring and Autumn period of Chinese history (722-488 BC), when various states vied for hegemony over the part of China north of the Yangtze River. Taking their ideas on statecraft and a philosophy of just and harmonious social relationships from one warring state to the next, Confucius and a small band of disciples sought to persuade each warlord prince that a doctrine based on worldly social-mindedness could provide stability and general well-being. But with the exception of the Duke of Zhou, no feudal overlord found Confucius relevant, practical or profound.

Confucius was more interested in educating than writing, and many of the ideas contained in the famous *Analects* were actually written by his devout followers. The dissemination of his thoughts was continued by succeeding generations of his disciples. During the Qin dynasty (221-207 BC), however, Confucianism was purged from the state ideology by the first unifier of China, Qin Shi Huangdi. An anti-intellectual and legalist who believed in the rule of laws, Qin made a practice of burning Confucian scholars along with their scrolls and brushes. Confucianism made a comeback during the Han dynasty (202 BC-220 AD), when Emporer Wu used it as his principal tool for controlling his subjects.

## The Patriarchal Family

Confucianism was at the centre of political and ideological life in China until 1905. That year, the civil service examination—the essential means of political advancement—was abolished in response to challenges for power from the imperialists and the clamor for more autonomous government from the merchant-gentry in the provinces. The death of Confucianism as the state ideology also signalled the downfall of the emperorship as the unifier of heaven, earth and people. As well, it destroyed the ruler's role as the symbolic father and mother of the Chinese people and as the son of heaven.

Confucian ideas on human relations and authority, however, lived on in most Chinese households. The family was considered a microcosm of society and the state, and harmony and stability had to prevail in each family unit in order to secure peace and continuity in the larger social and political arenas. The first rule of the Confucian family required that the oldest male be recognized as its head. The grandfather, typically the oldest living male, governed a patriarchal hierarchy that stressed the subordination of the son to the father, wife to the husband, younger brother to the older brother and in civil society, the subject to the ruler. Only in the relationship of friend and friend did the possibility of equality exist, but even this was tempered by considerations of age, class, social standing, education and marital status.

Confucian philosophy attached certain duties and patterns of behaviour to particular social roles, and stressed the need of each person to live according to his or her role. A harmonious family and a well-governed state could be attained only when "the prince [is] a prince, the minister a minister, the father a father and the son a son...for indeed when the prince is not a prince, the minister not a minister, the father not a father, the son not a son, one may have a dish of millet in front of one and yet not know if one will live to eat it."[1]

The authority of the oldest living male adult was upheld by the cardinal Confucian value, filial piety. "Never disobey!" was Confucius's advice to a young prince of the state of Lu unhappy about his parents' treatment of him.[2] If a son found himself disagreeing with his parents, he could at most "gently remonstrate with them. But if he sees that he has failed to change their opinion, he should resume an attitude of deference and not thwart them."[3]

"In serving his parents," according to the *Classic of Filial Piety*, "a filial son shows utmost reverence while at home, achieves utmost joy in supporting them, worries to the highest degree when they are sick, grieves to the utmost of their death and shows utmost gravity when sacrificing to them."[4]

Closely tied to the concept of filial piety was the practice of ancestor worship, a device to cope with the emotionally shattering and socially disintegrating event of the death of a family member.[5] Through ancestor worship, moral values such as filial piety were continued, especially for male heads of a household. Kinship values and family ties were bound ever tighter and chances of familial disintegration were reduced.

The authority of the oldest male adult, whose central purpose was to enrich the family and enhance its prosperity, gave him almost total control over the destiny of his immediate household and families related by kinship as well as those with clan ties. On the other side of the coin, his son had no latitude in choosing a career or a bride; everything—his education, vocation and marriage—was arranged. Only by marrying into a well-connected and prosperous family could a daughter contribute to the patriarchal family.

The rigid Confucian family was a reaction to unpredictable times in early China. The period was filled with war and civil chaos; the family, as the most intimate and human reflection of society and the state, had to be strong and stable where the larger society was not. When peace became the norm, the stability it brought with it was a boon to the Chinese family, giving many households the chance to prosper in the fields and marketplaces and to extend the lines of inheritance in the home. Social stability also loosened the reigns of the dictatorial authority of the oldest male adult in the family, who could afford to be less despotic and more benevolent.

## The Last Confucian Stronghold

Chinese families in the Americas did not enjoy the same stability and prosperity. The Chinese were a people wanted only for their strong backs, their market of 400 million customers, and the taxes, duties and profits they contributed to Gold Mountain. They were despised, shunned, and kept apart from the larger white community. The Chinese door-to-door vegetable peddler and laborer continually faced the threat of violent attacks by white toughs. City by-laws prohibiting the buying of property or the hiring of white help threatened to defeat the enterprises of Chinese merchants. Midnight police raids and arbitrary confiscation of goods became as commonplace and predictable in Chinatown life as Chinese opera on Saturday night. Because hostile outer forces prevented the Chinese from participating in the larger Canadian society, and after 1923 barred workers from even entering the country, those who elected to stay in Gold Mountain were forced to rely on their own time-tested survival techniques.

In times of instability in China, the Chinese patterned human relationships more strictly on Confucian ideas and values. Because white Canadians responded to the inhabitants of Chinatown with arrogance and hostility, the Chinese in North America turned to the traditional means of survival in a harsh and unpredictable environment.

In contrast to the Peking students and intellectuals of the famous May Fourth Movement of 1919 who questioned the relevance of Confucianism, the Chinese in North America faced a virtual state of seige and had little time for philosophical debate. Confucianism, as a tool of survival in the hostile New World, was never questioned. In Gold Mountain it remained pure in theory and application. While this New World Confucianism might be complemented by rituals and customs from other religions or ethical systems, it was never consumed by them. Buddhism and Christianity played a part in many lives, but because these dealt with the spiritual world, conflicts with Confucianism, which was essentially an earthly code of ethics rather than a religion, were minimal.

## Marriage in Gold Mountain

Confucianism viewed marriage as the most important event in a person's life. As the most intimate link between two families, a marriage not only solidified political affiliations and business partnerships, it was also the first step toward a continuation of the family line. Because of the need to ensure succession in a visibly unfriendly outer society, the stakes in a Chinese Canadian or Chinese American marriage were high, especially when women were scarce. Blunders resulting, for example, in a divorce without children could not be tolerated. The choice of groom and bride had to be carefully weighed. Custom and tradition carefully governed the process of selection, introduction, ceremony and post-nuptial obligations. Should the actual wedding ceremony contain elements of Christianity, it was at least partly regarded as a practical compromise within the tradition of the whole Confucian process of marriage: in Gold Mountain, a Christian marriage legitimized the union of two people in the eyes of the outer society.

In the traditional or Confucian marriage, the oldest living male adult decided the mate for the family's sons and daughters of marrying age. Implicit and expedient rules, rather than whimsy, dictated the choice. One consideration was the potential productivity of the woman in bearing children for the groom's household. For the bride's family, the social or monetary status of the new husband had to be taken into account. There were also political considerations on both sides. Nor could the father or grandfather consent to a marriage between a bride and groom with the same surname. Marriages between older women and younger men were frowned upon, especially when the woman was divorced or widowed. Another taboo was union with other races. These restrictions sometimes hindered the marriage process, but in a country where men outnumbered women by a large margin, the rules were often cast aside where the situation demanded. Until the 1923 exclusion act, some merchants bought wives and imported them from China.

In a community where great emphasis was placed on status and position and whose very survival called for caution and wisdom in the selection process, the matchmaker played an important role. While the matchmaker could be either male or female, professional or amateur, this position was most often filled by a woman noted for her acquaintance with many families. Although she received a *lisee** for her services, matchmaking was usually a sideline. But it was not a casual process; a matchmaker who brought about a liaison profitable to both sides and agreeable to the prospective bride and groom, reaped great social approval and recognition.

One of the most celebrated marriages in Victoria's Chinatown took place on August 8, 1932, when Chan Dun's son Steven took a bride from Vancouver. When Chan Dun launched his quest for a daughter-in-law, a matchmaker was summoned. The go-between was a Mrs. Lam, a close friend of Chan Dun's wife Koo Shee; the two had travelled from Hong Kong to Victoria on the same steamer in 1910.

Mrs. Lam was acquainted with Charlie Wing of Vancouver, whose family included three daughters. The eldest Wing daughter, Rosy, was a high school classmate of Mrs. Lam's daughter, and was known to be well educated and of sufficiently good character to marry Steven Chan, who at one time was a grammar school classmate of Mrs. Lam's son Andrew, later a well-known minister in the Winnipeg Chinese community. With these social ties reinforcing the prospects of a

*A small package, wrapped in red paper, containing money.

match, Mrs. Lam set the wheels in motion for a traditional Chinese wedding in Canada.

Friendship between Mrs. Lam, the Wing family and Mrs. Chan was not the only criterion for the match. Besides managing and owning the Panama Cafe, Chan Dun was also involved in the politics of China and was well known for his donations to the Guomindang. In 1912, he helped start a Chinese newspaper in Victoria supporting the Republic of China, the revolutionary government which replaced the Qing dynasty in 1911. Five years later, Chan Dun established a flying school to train aspiring Chinese pilots who would later fight for the republican cause in China.[6] In the course of these political activities, Chan Dun had often heard the passionate and persuasive oratory of Charlie Wing, the Vancouver tailor who had established himself as a strong supporter of the Guomindang.

With the additional ties of friendship and political bonds bringing the two families together, Mrs. Lam's next task was to arrange a meeting between the prospective couple. Her son Andrew was selected to accompany Steven to the Wing household on Union Street where the couple would be formally introduced.

While the prospective bride and groom did have some say in who they wanted as a mate, they could decide only within an arranged match sanctioned by their fathers. Before the first meeting of the prospective bride and groom, customarily the first stage in a traditional marriage, either household could break off negotiations without the loss of face. The concept of social embarrassment was so strong in Chinese tradition that a third party, the matchmaker, was essential in matters as delicate and important as marriage. If one household, for example, discovered through discussions with other friends, acquaintances or neighbors that the other family did not approach "the idea of a hardworking and domestically frugal household,"[7] the go-between was called in to sever the negotiations. She would tactfully suggest that "a marriage at this time would not be auspicious." Neither family would lose face, nor would they have to contend with social ridicule, as the two households had never faced one another in any of the marital negotiations.

### Betrothal

When each household was fully satisfied that the other was respectable, industrious and free from scandal, the prospective bride and groom were introduced by the matchmaker. If the man and woman appeared satisfied, an engagement announcement would then be circulated. In Victoria's Chinatown, where Chan Dun was a prominent figure, the betrothal of his son, who decided that a Vancouver bride was eminently suitable because her mother was some distance across the straits, was a special occasion in the life of a community based on the survival of merchant families.

At this time the groom's family symbolically "bought" the bride by giving her family some *lisee* packages. The act of "buying" emphasized the husband's position as the master in the new family and reinforced the authoritarian control of the oldest male adult on the groom's side—in this case, Chan Dun—over the bride and her children. This ritual illustrated the Confucian ethic of the "three bonds" that tied a woman to her father, husband and sons. The prospective bride was customarily also presented with a pair of bracelets, and the couple themselves often exchanged rings to symbolize their union and the union of their families.

Besides the price paid for the bride, agreed upon by both parties and paid by the groom's household at the time of the engagement, there were other traditional bridal demands: a roast pig, two live chickens, sweetmeats and assorted pastries and cookies had to be supplied by the groom's side. These were be distributed by the bride's family to neighbors, friends and kin, as part of the formal announcement of the upcoming event. Some of these meats were wrapped in the standard *lisee* packages with the character "double happiness" inscribed in gold ink. In the case of the Chan-Wing engagement, most of

Chinese railway workers, 1880s

One of the many bridges built by Chinese labor

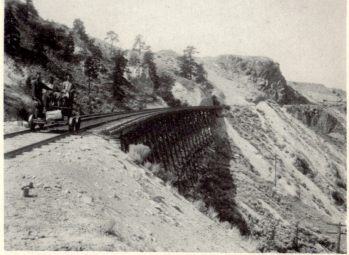

Merchant leaders in Victoria, 1925

Chan Dun, 1940s

The
Panama Cafe,
1940s

Right, the Chan children, Allan, Ira Esther, Phillip and Steven, 1917; below, Steven and Rosy Chan's wedding portrait; below right, Koo Shee's engagement photo, 1910

G. Lim Yuen, pastor of the Good Angel Mission in Vernon, B.C., with his family, 1920s.

Chinese school, Victoria, 1940s

The good Shepherd Mission, Vancouver, 1920s

the food was ordered from speciality shops in Vancouver's Chinatown and sent by courier to the bride's Union Street household.

## A Christian Wedding

Once it had been established that there would be a union of the Chan and Wing households Chan Dun, through Mrs. Lam, proposed to Charlie Wing that the wedding date be August 8, 1932. When this was agreed to, the pre-nuptial arrangements began in earnest. The matchmaker continued to play a pivotal role in conveying messages, settling misunderstandings and making certain that the schedule and customs be adhered to by both households. Such delicate matters as the bride price, or dowry, paid by the groom's household were handled by Mrs. Lam. She also handed out the guest list to both families, ensured that the dates of the banquets and of the wedding itself followed tradition, and made sure that the bride and groom were properly presented on the day of the wedding.

Both bride and groom had their hair cut and dressed before the wedding, a rite of passage symbolizing the transition from adolescence to adulthood; because the Chan-Wing marriage was a union of two twenty-year-olds, this ritual was merely symbolic.

The rituals leading up to the wedding—the introduction, the dressing of the hair—followed time-honored customs developed in southeastern China. The marriage ceremony itself, however, was a Western church service performed by a minister, in this case the Presbyterian minister Leang Wufong, who also served as the principal of the school on Fisgard Street where Chan Dun's children had learned Chinese.

The church itself was built with the help of donations from Chan Dun, whose own marriage to the missionary's daughter Koo Shee was solemnized by a Presbyterian minister, J.J. Campbell, on January 12, 1911.[8] Because the wedding was initiated by the groom's family, whose Christianity was well known in Victoria's Chinese community, it followed that the wedding itself be Christian.

The Christianizing of the Chinese in Canada had its roots in China after the Opium War of 1839-1842. Following in the footsteps of the Western merchants who coveted China's 400 million potential customers and natural resources, Western missionaries from all faiths, sects and beliefs swarmed into the treaty ports to save as many "heathen Chinee" as they could. Buying British tobacco, steam powered locomotives, woollens and armaments was not enough; the Chinese were to be sold a purifying Western creed to wrench them from the evils lurking in the Buddhist sutras, Moslem Koran, Confucian patriarchy and Daoist love of nature. In time, missionaries discovered that there were also Chinese non-believers in Canada, the United States and everywhere else Chinese people settled.

Sometimes Chinese converts would in turn bring others into the fold. One of these Chinese missionaries was G. Lim Yuen, pastor at the Good Angel Mission in Vernon, B.C.; another was Tom Chue Thom, who headed a Methodist church in New Westminster. By 1902, his church had 15 members, including two merchants. The night school provided lessons in English to 40 or 50 students, and 15 boys attended the public day school. Sixteen Chinese families were active in church activities.[9]

In Victoria, the education of Chinese children was provided by Chinese-language schools established as early as 1899.[10] Missionary and public schools taught in English. There were constant attempts by white Canadians to segregate the Chinese school children because of "the aptness of the Chinese to use words without knowing their meaning, and disregard for decency in giving expression in English to their lascivious thought."[11] Nonetheless, the sons and daughters of the Gold Mountain people managed to acquire education. But their education stopped at the boundaries of every Chinatown in Canada. Since the Chinese were not enfranchised until 1947, education beyond high school was impractical; many professions, including teaching, law and medicine, were restricted to Canadian citizens.

Employment restrictions almost always pushed the children

of cafe owners, laundry keepers and other petty merchants into their father's footsteps. As the wedding between the Chan and Wing households was being planned, it was absolutely certain that Steven would be a restaurant proprietor.

On August 8, 1932, the son of a cafe owner and the daughter of a tailor from Vancouver were married according to the rituals of the Presbyterian church. In many ways, the influence of the Christian religion drew the Chan family and other Chinese households like them into a sacred area of Canadian life. They believed in a Western God and were convinced that the Messiah and the church were integral parts of their spiritual well-being. Because Chan Dun and other Christian merchants and laborers contributed to the growth of Christianity in the Chinese community by their hard work, cash donations, and service as officers in the church hierarchy, they—unlike some converts in China who adopted a Western religion in exchange for food and privileges—were committed to their religious beliefs.

By calling on the Christian church to sanction such an important event in the lives of the Chan and Wing families, Chan Dun largely turned his back on the Confucian marriage ritual. There were no signs of the traditional large red marriage candles in either home on the night before the wedding. In the altar of the bride's household, a paper image of a dragon symbolizing masculinity would have accompanied the burning of these candles. The groom's house would also have candles, but with an image of a phoenix, symbolizing femininity. Both parties would have been required to wear special white cotton suits until the night of consummation following the wedding.[12]

A traditional marriage would also have seen the bride and groom paying their respects to the sacred objects and memories of the groom's household. These included bowing "to the house dieties, to Heaven and Earth, to the ancestors of the house, and to the groom's seniors."[13] This special bridal entry into the groom's household symbolized the beginning of life in her husband's family; it was the first initiation rite of the bride as a married woman.

113

Use of the Christian marriage ceremony did not in fact contradict the family's acceptance of traditional Confucian values. Because the Chinese view of life involved many highly integrated facets, a person's earthly existence complemented and co-existed with the religious and spiritual aspects of one's life. A family in the southwest province of Yunnan could be Confucian, yet still look to Mecca for spiritual salvation. Buddhism and Daoism also played a significant role in the lives of the Chinese. But because these religions were thought to concern themselves with a separate, non-social, non-political sphere, they were not a threat to the values and customs of Confucianism. Religions and perspectives on life and death of all shades could exist side-by-side with Confucianism and its emphasis on human relationships in the here and now. Religious tolerance was the norm in Chinese culture. Until the advent of Christianity, the bloody religious crusades found in the histories of France, England, Spain and the Middle East did not blight China. Because of the Confucian accommodation of different schools of thought, Christianity could live and even flourish in a Confucian environment. But once Christianity attempted to destroy the Confucian order by replacing it with its own set of ethical and earthly values, the Confucian harmony of opposites ceased to exist. The most infamous Christian attempt to "save" the Chinese people occurred during the Taiping Rebellion, which left more than twenty million dead in fourteen years.

While Christianity played a significant role in the marriages of Chan Dun in 1910 and of his son in 1932, it did not affect the Confucian pattern of social relations between father and son, elder and younger brother, husband and wife, and friend and friend. Nor did it alter the traditional relationship between the political leader (emperor, president or prime minister) and subject. If anything, Christianity, with its stress on church dogma, reliance on a strict hierarchy, and inequality between men and women, actually complemented the feudal structure of Confucianism.

What Christianity did accomplish in Chinese communities in

Canada was the elimination of concubinage. Though it failed to change the patriarchal wife-husband relationship, it did eliminate polygamy and child brides, and ancestor worship became less important. Christianity could also bring the Chinese closer to the mainstream of Canadian life, but discriminatory laws, the lack of the franchise, and segregation by white Canadians ruled out full participation as a Canadian citizen with equal rights and opportunities.

Chan Dun and other Chinese household heads decided to give their children a Christian wedding, not in an effort to enhance their standing in the eyes of a hostile community, but because of sincerely held beliefs. Christianity sanctioned the Chan-Wing wedding; it made the union blessed in the realm of God and legal in the dusty columns of the government's marriage registry.

After the Christian ceremony, Confucian customs prevailed at the celebrations. There were traditional banquets at which *lisee* packages were distributed to younger siblings. Family friends, kin and clan members joined together in celebration. Two of the three banquets were scheduled for the same time, five o'clock on the wedding day, for extended family and friends. Because Chan Dun's Panama Cafe was once a three-storey vaudeville theatre, he was able to set aside the second floor for one feast. Manyin Low, one of Victoria's best Chinese caterers, set ten tables at a cost of $8 each for 100 women and their children. At the same time the men celebrated at the Peking Restaurant, where a more elaborate and sumptuous meal, accompanied by fine liquor, was ordered for ten tables; here the cost was $15 to $20 per table. About 100 close family friends, cronies and business associates joined Chan Dun in the celebration.

Now that Chan Dun's eldest son had married, the younger siblings were free to wed once they reached the proper age. This was the usual custom in Cantonese marriages; the aim was to ensure continuity in succession. If a younger son was able to persuade his father that his marriage would enhance the family's fortune even though his older brother had not yet married, he could do so but his wife would still be the junior daughter-in-law. By the same token, daughters were also required by custom to marry by seniority. Again, this could be sidestepped if a younger daughter was to marry a wealthy merchant or powerful politician who would bring prestige and fortune to her family. In Gold Mountain, where men outnumbered women by a wide margin, seniority was adhered to only when it did not hinder the growth of the family.

The custom of segregating women and men on important occasions such as a wedding celebration was not always strictly observed. The bridal couple, though, was obliged to toast each banquet table in both the men's and women's sections. In turn, the guests made a toast to the couple, wishing them good health, prosperity, happiness, fecundity and longevity. Each guest also passed a *lisee* to the pair. With twenty tables to cover, the newly wed Chans indulged in nothing stronger than weak tea.

Finally, on the morning following the wedding, the groom's household once again sent a roast pig, two live chickens, liquor, oranges, pastries and cookies to the bride's family. In the Cantonese tradition, this array was not simply a show of congratulations or gratitude. It carried a more serious, and potentially unpleasant, message. While the bride's chastity was usually taken for granted by the time the engagement and bridal price had been agreed upon, there was always a chance that she might not be as "pure" as both families had believed. If this was thought to be the case, the groom's family had to safeguard their integrity and reputation. This was symbolically achieved by slicing off a pig's ear or tail and sending the mutilated carcass, along with the other foods still intact, to the bride's family. This public demonstration of the bride's unsuitability conveyed an unequivocal statement: the contract of marriage was hereby terminated.[14] This action was almost based on the Western business motto, "Satisfaction guaranteed or your money refunded." In this case, the Chans were satisfied and the Wings were able to enjoy the delicacies.

### Bridal Induction

The Chan-Wing wedding was completed on the morning of August 9, 1932. The final ritual of bridal induction took place at the Panama. Known as the *jumcha*, or the rite of pouring tea, this was the first meeting between the bride and the groom's extended family. The women in the household received tea poured by the bride. With each cup poured, a *lisee* was passed to the bride. This tea ceremony demonstrated the new bride's respect for the women in her husband's extended family—the people with whom she would come into daily contact. More importantly, she was now formally welcomed into her new household. This marked her transition from her own family in which she was raised from birth to attachment to the family in which she was expected to begin her adulthood. Later that night, the Chan household celebrated the marriage with its third and final feast, reserved for extended family members.

Finally, the new couple was to visit the bride's family. Accompanying them was the third and final array of foods, again delivered by courier from speciality shops in Vancouver's Chinatown. This visit was the official announcement to the bride's family that she was now a member of her new husband's household.

### Gold Mountain Village

Chinese weddings in Canada were cause for great celebration because they added to the prosperity and cohesiveness of the community. Each marriage and each Chinese baby born on Canadian soil strengthened the community's chances of survival. Still, to Chinese children, growing up in Canada meant growing up in Chinatown, with its streets for a playground and a favorite grandparent for advice and comfort. The future was often one of menial labor at their father's shop or cafe, Chinese classes after public school, and little hope of opportunity for moving up in the world.

Ostracized by white Canadian society with its discriminatory legislation and racist attitudes, the people of Gold Mountain developed their own self-sufficient and self-generating urban villages. As in China during the Yuan, Qing and Republican (1912-1949) periods, those who prescribed the rules governing the daily lives of the Chinese were not themselves Chinese. In the Americas, officials declared that the Chinese were aliens, outsiders; the Chinese, they said, did not have the mental and physical attributes to become Canadian or American citizens. The evidence was China itself, with its millions living in poverty, backwardness, dictatorship and paganism. China was unable to contain the onslaught of Western marauders, cut-throats and drug dealers because its people were simply "unfit."

As did the Chinese during the Yuan, Qing and the Republican periods, the Chinese in Gold Mountain looked inward for survival. Forced into bowing their heads and paying taxes to foreigners, the men and women of Gold Mountain built around themselves an elaborate community that resembled the village network of southeastern China. Unlike some ghettoes in Western cities that nourished poverty and despair, Chinatowns were vibrant urban villages struggling to develop under the weight of a hostile outer society. Like the Chinese village, North American Chinatown was divided into two classes: the rich and the poor.

A major difference between Chinatown and the Chinese village was the social position of the merchants. In China, merchants occupied the bottom rung of the social ladder, beneath artisans, peasants and the scholar-gentry. In Gold Mountain, on the other hand, the daily struggle for physical survival did not allow the existence of a leisure class occupying its time with study, reflection and examination-writing, until the middle of the twentieth century. Frontier North America needed industrious and strong people with intelligence to overcome Western bigotry and internal bickering. Placed in a society that extolled free enterprise, Chinese merchants in the Americas rose to the top of the social scale in their own communities. Their affluence in turn gave them the time to dabble in calligraphy, Buddhism and philanthropic works, formerly the province of the landed gentry. Merchants also developed a knowledge of kinship organization and established such groups as the Hoy Sun Ning Benevolent Association (Taishan Association). They set up social welfare agencies such as the Chinese Consolidated Benevolent Association. Institutions like these were expressions of the merchant class's role as a pillar of the Chinese community. They also initiated schools, set up credit associations, and perpetuated tradition and custom, all lending stability to a growing community. Later they would adopt Western music, reading habits and manners.

Features of North American Chinese communities—the division between merchants and laborers, the gentry-like obligations of the merchants, and the importance of Confucianism in human relations—closely paralleled the main features of a rural village society in Guangdong province in China. In a land called Gold Mountain, the village ways of doing things were frozen in time and space. Because of their exclusion from North American society, the thoughts and actions of the Gold Mountain people were directed towards the Chinese communities nestled in other cities across North America and in China, Hong Kong and Southeast Asia. What touched the people of China touched the lives of the Chinese in the Americas. The special foods, the old ways of marrying, the unique customs of friendship and the politics of China were an inseparable part of life in the urban villages in Gold Mountain.

# Escape From the Empire

The people of Gold Mountain were provided a window to the outside world and to a more dynamic political tradition by the presence in their midst of exiles from China—rebels, revolutionaries and reformers. They were adventurers, gamblers and individuals of idealism and conscience whose principles or thirst for power sealed their fate in the eyes of the Chinese government. With a price on their heads and a place on Peking's most-wanted lists, these political refugees formed a constantly mobile segment of the Chinatown population. Unlike the womanless workers in the railway camps, laundries, mines or canneries, or the sober merchant with his family in Canada, these political exiles were true sojourners who viewed their time in Gold Mountain as a brief interlude before an ocean liner took them back to their war against, at first, the Qing dynasty and when that was overthrown in 1911, the Chinese warlords.

Living a shifting, transient life, these exiles constantly hungered for news from China. Often pursued by Chinese government assassins, they were men on the run. Their posture was one of distrust and suspicion. But in their quest for political donations, allies and refuge, they won the allegiance of merchants and laborers alike. They linked the two classes in the common goal of expelling the foreign Manchus and later the military juntas from their homeland.

Guangdong, where most Gold Mountain Chinese came, had for many centuries provided refuge to the enemies of the Chinese throne. Before the Tang dynasty annexed Guangdong and its chief city, Canton, disgraced officials, rebels and political pariahs fled to the southernmost provinces. There, they sought protection and time for planning future assaults on the government.

After South China became incorporated into the empire, rebels and political outcasts looked to the south seas and what is now known as Southeast Asia for refuge; with the advent of the Tang dynasty, Canton became the Chinese port of call for foreign entrepreneurs from the south and, at the same time, the first port of flight for dissidents and those accused of treason and sedition fleeing China.[1]

Every time a dynasty fell, more peasant victims of the civil wars as well as officials of the fallen government fled to South China, some eventually heading for the south seas via Canton. During the Ming dynasty, Cantonese officials processed many immigrant exiles from Fujian, Guangxi and Guangdong on ships leaving for Nanyang. When the Manchus overthrew the Ming dynasty in 1655, the famous Ming patriot Koxinga, or Zheng Chenggong, fled to Taiwan but maintained an active resistance network in Fujian. Since he had widespread support from the anti-Manchu populace on the coasts of Zhejiang, Fujian and Guangdong, the Qing government sent its troops to kill off Ming sympathizers and burn the villages and food supplies from the beaches to 30 miles inland of these provinces. Their homes destroyed, the only alternative for the survivors was emigration and exile in an alien land.[2]

Chinese North America was a community of social networks that crossed international boundaries and brought the Chinese people together in a complex array of kinship, clan, regional

121

and provincial ties. The distinction between Canada and the United States was not always recognized; a Vancouver cannery worker writing to his peasant family in Taishan would not refer to Canada but to Gold Mountain, just as another family in the same district might hear from their relatives in San Francisco who would talk of Gold Mountain but not about *Meiguo* (America).

Racist attitudes of the white population helped crystallize Chinese North America into a cohesive community, but perhaps the strongest glue was the community's passionate interest in the affairs and politics of China. While interest was shared, views often were not; the subject was guaranteed to inflame passions and to pit brother against brother, neighbor against neighbor. The politics of China permeated Gold Mountain life; the Chinese were among the most politicized people in Canada.

The fact that most Chinese came from southern China and not central or northern China largely determined the nature of Chinese politics in Gold Mountain. Taiping rebels, pushed southward by Manchu troops and their Western imperialist allies after the fall of Nanjing in 1864, headed for Canton and on to Southeast Asia or the Americas. Their presence in Guangxi and Guangdong turned South China into a mecca of dissident ideas and activities. Out of this political environment came the Chinese merchants and laborers eager to make a living across the Pacific. In their travels to the New World, rebels and emigrants used traditional associations, or Triad societies, as a bridge across the sea.[3]

The Triads, which included the *Tiandi hui* (Heaven and Earth Society), *Santian hui* (Triple Dot Society) and the *Sanhe hui* (Triple Unit Society) and various other branches, were known by southern Chinese and the Cantonese in particular as the *Hongmen*, or "the vast gate."[4] In Canada, the Triads were also known as the Chikongtang.

Originally operating in Zhejiang, Fujian and Taiwan, the Triads placed a mystical significance on the number three and referred to the interchange between heaven, earth and people.

Closely associated with the legend of the Shaolin monks and their skill at martial arts (*gongfu*), the Triads' major political purpose was to overthrow the Qing dynasty and restore the Ming (*fanqing fuming*) to the throne. By the nineteenth century its rebellious activities had quickened into political uprisings in Jiangxi, Guangxi, Hunan and Guangdong.

As a result of the imperialist surge that began with the Opium War in 1839, China's economy became more and more dependent on the West. The jobless rate accelerated, and workers looked overseas for new opportunities. Emigration increased with the movement of people to Southeast Asia and the Americas. Triad branches accompanied this flight from poverty and misery, and the politics of China came as the cultural baggage of the secret society members.[5] The people of Gold Mountain would escape neither the movements to destroy the Qing dynasty nor the rhetoric and solicitations of the famous Sun Yat-sen.

### Exiles in Canada

Of all the revolutionary exiles, Sun Yat-sen was the most revered in overseas Chinese communities. Although he was in Denver, Colorado on a fund-raising tour when the revolution toppled the Qing emperor and installed Yuan Shikai as the first head of the infant republic, Sun was seen as the father of the Chinese revolution. It was his style that set the tone of the upheaval and subsequent new order, and it was his optimism and rapport with the Chinese in Gold Mountain that gave a sense of purpose to a people snubbed in their hostile new home. Sun typified persistence against heavy odds and exuded confidence that goals were attainable through hard work. These were the very traits that described the people of Gold Mountain. His fight was theirs, and his victory was proof that their own struggle in North America against injustice and exploitation could succeed. These were the reasons that shopkeepers like Charlie Wing, cafe owners like Chan Dun, and other merchants and laborers supported Sun's dream of a

China ruled by the Chinese.

Sun came to Victoria in 1897 to solicit funds and establish contacts among the people of Chinatown. At first, the merchants were lukewarm to Sun's overtures. There were other groups contending for their hearts and pocketbooks, and some sections of the community found it safer and more pragmatic to support the reform efforts of the famous Confucian scholar Kang Youwei than the revolutionary cause of Sun.

Kang made contacts with the Chinese in Canada in 1899, a year after he and his disciple Liang Qichao had escaped Qing assassins. Like Sun, Kang wanted the funds and support of wealthy overseas Chinese. Like Sun, he also had a price on his head. But unlike Sun, who wanted a revolution and a republic, Kang called for a constitutional monarchy based on a Confucian model of government.[6]

Kang's prestige as a scholar mesmerized many in Gold Mountain, and a branch of his Protect the Emperor Society (*Baohuanghui*) was established on July 20, 1899, with $7,900 in donations.[7] During the Boxer uprising in 1900, the secretary of the Vancouver *Baohuanghui*, Won Alexander Cumyow, announced that his group would send a force of Chinatown volunteers to save the Emperor from the notorious Empress Dowager, Ci Xi (this was mere rhetoric; soldiers were never sent).[8]

Kang Youwei again visited Victoria and Vancouver in 1902. In 1904 his Chinatown lieutenants presented him with a membership list of 7,000 in twelve local branches across Canada. However, dissent split the ranks of his followers, and by 1905 Sun had set up his Alliance League (*Tongmeng hui*), a powerful challenge to the *Baohuanghui*,[9] which ceased to exist after the 1911 revolution. The coffers of the overseas Chinese were now ripe for Sun's picking.

Sun Yat-sen's pitch to the people of Gold Mountain was his promise of an imminent revolutionary victory and of subsequent investment opportunities in China.[10] He also pledged to give special consideration in his post-war government to those who contributed to the cause during the period of struggle; contributors would be declared "preferential citizens" who could become citizens of the new Republic of China without going through whatever citizenship hurdles the new government decided upon for others.[11]

The chance to reap immense profits from a republic that was not yet born, however, was not always enough to loosen the purse strings of prosperous merchants, whose savings were the result of conservative and cautious investments. The fatherland, China, under the yoke of alien domination and subjugation—that was the emotional tug that loosened the purse strings of merchants and workers. At the centre of this Chinese nationalism was the Triad Society. Its members kept alive the idea of a China ruled by and for Chinese people in their speeches to laborers in rail camps, merchants in association halls, and in public places where the people of Gold Mountain worked and lived.

Secret society members prepared the way for Sun Yat-sen's visits to Victoria and Vancouver. On his third visit in 1911 to Vancouver, a crowd of more than 1,000 welcomed him as he descended from his railway car. He spoke daily on the revolutionary cause to packed houses of 1,000 at a Chinese theatre.[12] By now, the idea of a new republic had caught the imagination of many Chinese outside of China. The main reasons for this were Sun's organizing abilities and his charismatic persona. His presence could silence a room and he could sway a dubious audience with his fire and conviction.

When members of the Qing government's New Army staged a coup d'etat in Wuchang on October 10, 1911, and established the revolutionary government, the allegiance of merchant and worker in Gold Mountain was consolidated. In 1912, Seto Maytong, a *Hongmen* official, raised $150,000 for the new republic by mortgaging the society's buildings in Victoria, Vancouver and Toronto. This large donation dwarfed the contributions made when the revolution was still a dream. In 1897, merchants and workers gave Sun enough funds to travel first class on the *Empress of India* bound for China from Vancouver. By the spring of 1911, HK$70,000 was subscribed by *Hongmen* members through mortgages on their clubhouses to buy "patriotic" bonds for the revolution. An additional $85,000 had been raised in Canada by the people of Chinatown for the abortive April 27, 1911, rebellion near Canton (72 revolutionaries were killed; the incident is marked by a memorial at the site, a village north of Canton, called Huanhuagang[13]).

The Qing government's enemies were not the only ones seeking support in Gold Mountain; the Qing government itself tried to win over the people of Gold Mountain and their pocketbooks. Like Sun Yat-sen, its agents dangled the lure of investment possibilities in a modern China. It bolstered this argument by pointing to the inability of merchants to invest in their own countries because of the racism and discriminatory practices of the white population.[14] Overseas Chinese merchants were reminded that they did not have access to symbols of status or prestige in Canada.

The Qing court offered to sell them official titles of the empire. It also encouraged them to observe the emperor's birthday and to welcome high-ranking visitors from China. On paper, the Qing government showed its support for the activities (especially the business activities) of the overseas communities by ending its ban on emigration from China in 1893 and sending its representatives to champion the cause of overseas Chinese.[15]

This shift in Peking's attitude toward the overseas Chinese actually began years earlier, during the 1870s, when China was undergoing a period of reconstruction after the Taiping Rebellion. Tales of wealthy overseas merchants reached the ears of Qing officials who needed ready cash to rebuild the country and to modernize it with Western technology. What eventually flourished in government circles was the myth that China could save itself merely by reaching out to the pocketbooks and commercial experience of the overseas merchants.[16] People who were once considered political pariahs and traitors because they emigrated to escape poverty and misery were now feted and cajoled, their patriotism appealed to.[17] For a while, this campaign to gain overseas support worked. Many entrepreneurs and laborers sent money for flood and drought relief, bought titles and welcomed emissaries from China to their shores.

The first visit of a Qing dignitary to Canada was that of Li Hongzhang in 1896. The purpose of his tour was to show the Chinese of Gold Mountain that the Qing court sympathized with them in their plight, and to scout the actual material wealth of the overseas Chinese. In 1908, the Qing government again showed its concern for their "patriots" overseas by sending Li Qinggui to head an educational commission inspecting the new Chinese schools in Victoria and Vancouver. His purpose was to encourage the education of Chinese children in the Chinese language. In the same year, a consulate was finally established in Ottawa.[18]

The Qing government's attitude towards the overseas Chinese was also reflected in its reference to its emigrants as *huaren* (Chinese people) or *huamin* (Chinese) in official documents after 1876. The bureaucrat responsible for the change was the governor-general of Guangdong and Guangxi, Liu Kunyi.[19] The Chinese in Gold Mountain and elsewhere now had a particular status as actual people; no longer were they were counter-revolutionary rabble.


## Still The Sojourner!

After elevating them from the ranks of non-people, the Qing government tried to defend its newly designated "patriots" by issuing declarations and protests against racist legislation in Gold Mountain. It also attempted to destroy the undeserved myth that the Chinese merely wanted to milk Canada of its riches before scurrying back to China to live in ease and comfort. This notion of the Chinese was set out by Prime Minister John A. Macdonald, who in 1882 told his colleagues in parliament that the Chinese were unlikely to remain as permanent settlers because they brought neither wives nor children.[20] He said they were transients or sojourners whose only role in Canada was to use their muscle and strong backs in the aid of frontier progress. As this myth of the sojourner gradually took hold in the imagination of the white populace, it became easier to deport and harass a people who supposedly never wanted to stay on and build a life as Canadian citizens anyway.

Exclusionists also pointed to large financial donations Chinese made to political causes in China; this proved to them that the Chinese never wanted to remain in Canada, and looked to China for their political interests. Yet few Chinese actually saw themselves as mere sojourners. Even the Chinese government recognized that, with few exceptions, emigrants to the Americas moved there with the intention of staying. In 1885, the San Francisco-based Qing consul-general Huang Cunxian told a Royal Commission into Chinese immigration:

> ...it is charged that the Chinese do not emigrate to foreign countries to remain, but only to earn a sum of money and return to their homes in China. It is only about thirty years since our people commenced emigrating to other lands. A large number have gone to the Straits' Settlements, Manila, Cochin China and the West India Islands, and are permanently settled there with their families. In Cuba, fully seventy-five per cent have married native women and adopted those Islands as their future homes. Many of those living in the Sandwich Islands have done the same....
>
> There is quite a large number of foreigners in China, but few of whom have brought their families, and the number is very small indeed who have adopted that country as their future home.
>
> You must recollect that the Chinese immigrant coming to this country is denied all the rights and privileges extended to others in the way of citizenship; the laws compel them to remain aliens.
>
> I know a great many Chinese will be glad to remain here permanently with their families, if they are allowed to be

naturalized and can enjoy privileges and rights.[21]

Huang Cunxian's comments did not dissuade the Canadian government from imposing head taxes, which reached their peak at $500 in 1904. This levy effectively prevented laborers, who were typically making $25 a month, from sending for their wives and children. A merchant like Chan Dun, however, could reach into his savings to pay the tax and have his fiancee Koo Shee enter Canada. Others, like the market gardener Sing Cheung Yung, could probably afford to bring his family from China, but Sing decided that "the people in this country talk so much against the Chinese that I don't care to bring them here."[22] Head taxes were also levied against Chinese students, who had to pay $350 on arrival in Canada. The money would be returned once the student had completed one year of study in Canada.[23]

The Chinese government lodged protests with Canada through the British Foreign Office.[24] In 1909, Peking's acting foreign office head, Liang Tunyen, told W.L. Mackenzie King, then Canada's deputy labor minister, that China "adhered to its traditional policy of discouraging contract labor while acting on the principle that there be a liberty of movement for free laborers." Liang also protested the imposition of Canada's head taxes.[25]

King's reply suggested that Canada was doing China a favor by instituting this notorious levy; he said that the head tax "stood, to appearances, as a mark against the Chinese. The tax, however, had been imposed not with this object, but to effect the restriction of a certain class, without going the length of exclusion." He continued that as the "number paying the tax increased, it became a considerable revenue, but the tax was never intended as revenue."[26]

Despite King's protest that the head taxes were never intended as revenue, 47,342 Chinese immigrants to Canada from January 1, 1885, to August 31, 1908, filled Ottawa's coffers with a total of $4,381,550. Immigration was drastically reduced when the last increase, to $500, came into effect, but the 2,698 immigrants who arrived in Canada from that date until April 31, 1908, did pay Ottawa $1,349,000 for the privilege of living in Gold Mountain.[27]

The $500 head tax was a crushing blow to the hopes of laborers and poor shopkeepers who wanted to bring their wives and children to Canada. Without families, many bachelor workers and small merchants had no alternative but to carry on with their life of gambling, drugs and occasional visits to a brothel. Still, their most serious interests were in the politics of China, which they followed with dedication. Denied the right to vote in a democratic country and, therefore, the right to participate in normal political activities, they earnestly pursued and supported one faction or another in China.

### The Revolution in Canada

When the Qing dynasty abdicated on February 12, 1912, the struggle for the revolution appeared to be over. Anti-Manchu groups coalesced into one party supporting the republic. In Gold Mountain there was jubilation at the fall of an imperial system that had ruled China since 221 BC. Sun Yat-sen and his supporters had triumphed. But by February, 1912, Yuan Shikai emerged as the power behind the revolution; he gained control of the government and the northern army. Supported by the imperialists,[28] this former civil servant of the Qing court and confidante of the late Empress Dowager Ci Xi shunted Sun off to the post of Director of Railway Development.

Sun took this post because he felt that he could still play off Yuan and serve China at the same time. Besides, Yuan's offer was made amid a warm and generous welcome that included royal honors and a lavish apartment for Sun's stay in Peking between August 24 and September 20, 1912. Sun, the consummate rebel and a thorn in the Manchu side for almost two decades, was even given an elaborate feast by one of the princes. Victory was still in the air and its euphoric after-effects brought together the strangest bedfellows. It was a moment in which to savour the revolution, heal old wounds and unite under one common banner.

Sun's time as an underling in Yuan Shikai's government lasted until April 26, 1913, when he protested the way in which Yuan masterminded the Reorganization Loan of 25 million pounds from a consortium of imperialist bankers.[29] His final break with the Peking government came when he learned that Yuan had a hand in the death of a promising republican named Song Jiaoren. By the spring of 1914, Sun Yat-sen was again on the run, in search of donations to finance a second revolution. Once more he turned to the Chinese outside of China for support.

Although he was never again to visit Canada, the people of Gold Mountain remembered him and his revolutionary cause. Their faith in a new Republic of China was manifested by cash donations and participation in Sun's new party, formed out of the Alliance League and other groups on August 25, 1912. Called the Nationalist Party or the Guomindang, this new revolutionary vehicle rallied broad support. In 1913, following a campaign based on honesty and high principles, the Guomindang scored a spectacular victory in China's first ever national election by taking 360 of 500 seats in the house of representatives.[30] It was becoming such a political force that Yuan Shikai initiated the Reorganization Loan to finance a military campaign against the Guomindang that year.

The Guomindang's propaganda organ in Canada was the *Sunmin kwokbao* (*Xinmin guobao*) or the *New Republican Tabloid*, published in Victoria. One of the merchants who had a hand in its establishment was Chan Dun, who typified the small merchant and shopkeeper's commitment to the republican revolution. In 1917, he translated his republican leanings into support for the Guomindang by setting up aviation schools in the Willows Beach area in Victoria and in Esquimalt to train Sun Yat-sen's revolutionary pilots. Chan Dun was the principal of the enterprise, but the training was co-ordinated by a Captain Brown.[31]

One of the far-reaching battles in the Chinese community centred on the competition between the Guomindang and the

Chikongtang for control of the Chinese Consolidated Benevolent Association. The CBA saw itself as the national voice of the Chinese in Canada, even though some cities with a sizeable Chinese population such as Calgary did not have a chapter until the 1930s.[32] But because it was well established in the major cities—Victoria, Vancouver, Montreal and Toronto—it achieved credibility as a national organization. Whoever controlled it, the Guomindang or the Chikongtang (now known as the Chinese Freemasons), was the powerhouse in Chinatown politics. This factional war was further complicated by the Freemasons' bitterness towards Sun Yat-sen whom it helped considerably with donations, contacts and arms during its days as a secret society. Sun's establishment of the Guomindang as his primary political machine was taken as a slap in the face by the Freemasons' leaders, who expected rewards and favors for their part in the successful revolution.

By the 1920s, the Freemasons had entered into a common front with the *Baohuanghui*, now resurrected as the Constitutional Party.[33] But with the appearance on the Chinese political scene of the Soviet Union and the Chinese Communist Party in 1924, the insular Chinatown conflict escalated into an ideological fight that endures today. The Guomindang-Freemasons battle turned out to be a mere preliminary to the main event.

Meanwhile, a clandestine gun-running network was supporting the revolutionaries and the Guomindang by smuggling pistols (the automatic pistol was the most popular), machine guns and other arms from Canada through Hong Kong into South China. The go-betweens were Chinese sailors or ship workers, whose constant travel across the Pacific made gun smuggling relatively easy and profitable. Their activities, however, were well known to the Canadian authorities. In December, 1919, the Northwest Mounted Police discovered, through a Chinatown informer, a lively traffic in small arms on Canadian Pacific ships plying their way to China.[34]

One of the most illustrious gun-runners in Victoria was Y. George Lee Kun, a graduate of Victoria High School who bought and sold arms for the revolutionary cause. His shipment of half a million Chinese dollars' worth of handguns to Canton in 1921 was his biggest deal.[35] That same year, a merchant named Chin Pai-pong operated a flourishing armaments syndicate out of Vancouver. Arms were bought from cartels in the United States for US$24 and repackaged and sold to the Chinese for US$200. Chin's chief backers were various merchants in Victoria's Chinatown. In one investment, he secured $1,152.50, half from a Don Yuen.[36]

Even though it was relatively easy to conceal handguns in packages of clothing, kegs of nails or among boxes of household goods, careless smugglers in Hong Kong often found themselves facing fines of up to HK$100 or twelve months of hard labor or both. The punishment was sometimes supplemented by ten or twelve strokes of the cane.[37] The risks, however, were small compared to the potential profits.

## After Exclusion

Developments in China continued to influence the course of politics in Gold Mountain even after Ottawa closed the door of entry to many Chinese immigrants in 1923. As long as ships crossed the Pacific, Chinese workers would smuggle Western arms and contraband into the chaotic arena of Chinese politics. After 1924, the Guomindang began to reorganize with the help of the Chinese Communists, and the contest for control of China gradually began to include Sun Yat-sen's party. In 1928, when Sun's successor Chiang Kai-shek took over Peking with the help of some disaffected warlords, the stakes in China became ideological as well as military. By the 1930s the Communists, on the run since 1927 after their break with the Guomindang, replaced the republican loyalist warlords as Chiang Kai-shek's principle enemy.

In Canada, the Guomindang became the strongest force in Chinatown politics. Although forced underground between September, 1918, and May, 1919, because Ottawa had banned its activities under pressure from the warlord government in

Peking, the Guomindang faction never lost its prevalent position. In 1928, when Japanese and Western imperialists recognized the Guomindang, headquartered at Nanking, as the legitimate government of China, its esteem and prestige blossomed further in Gold Mountain. But just as factions like the Freemasons kept the Guomindang from complete domination of Chinatown, the party in China came under attack from warlords in Yunnan, Sichuan and other provinces as well as from Communist insurgents. The party's credibility declined and its widespread corruption and exploitation were increasingly evident to the Chinese people. With its weak leadership and fascist tendencies, Guomindang domination of Chinese and Gold Mountain politics was to be precarious and brittle.

The year 1929 saw the Toronto chapter of the Guomindang in the midst of a ferocious battle with the Freemasons. Attacking the economic lifeline of its rivals, the Guomindang called on the Toronto police to raid certain Freemason gambling houses, widely known in Chinatown as money-making operations. The local gendarmerie was only too happy to oblige, and raids were conducted during 1929 and 1930; in one month alone, 90 raids were recorded. By 1941 the Guomindang in Toronto was able to pass itself off as the voice of Toronto's Chinese community. In fact, that year Toronto's city council, wishing to stop illegal liquor sales by Chinese businesses to white minors, did so by asking the Guomindang to police its own constituency. The sales stopped.[38]

The internal battle for control of the CBA cooled in 1942 with the establishment of a coalition to run the organization. Included in the coalition were representatives from the Guomindang, the Freemasons and a third bloc of executives representing the Wong (Wang) and Hoysun Ningyung Benevolent Associations.[39] There was actually considerable overlap in memberships; Chan Dun, for example, was a card-carrying Guomindang as well as a member of the Hoysun Ningyun association.

After Pearl Harbor, Guomindang China became part of the

Allied "big four" that included the Soviet Union, Britain, and the United States. Such an exalted position in global affairs naturally had its spin-offs in the Chinatowns across the world. On the big screen in Gold Mountain theatres, the Chinese were depicted as heroic figures defending their country against the rapacious Japanese.[40] For once it was good to be Chinese, to be fighting alongside the Americans while other Asians in the Americas were incarcerated for looking like the enemy from the island kingdom. Some Chinese even took to sporting badges declaring "I'm Chinese, Not a Jap!"

But when the war ended, China once again assumed its real role, as a colony of the Western powers. By 1945, when China was plunged into the civil war between Zhu De's Red Army and the American-backed Guomindang forces, Chiang Kai-shek had little grass-roots support. Eventually, Mao Zedong's disciplined army proved far superior to the Nationalist forces, which hastily retreated to Taiwan. When liberation arrived in the summer of 1949, the Chinese seized their country back from the foreign powers which dominated it. The Americans spoke resentfully of how China had been "lost," as if it was a piece of property owned by the United States. Like a parent reclaiming a lost child from foreign abductors just at the moment of the child's maturity, the Chinese reasserted their right to rule their country as a sovereign state. The victory by Mao and Zhu dashed all hopes Washington had for a pliable Chinese regime "allied with the United States and exercising a stabilizing influence upon Asia."[41] There was much hand-wringing over losing a pivotal country on the threshold of becoming a "strong, unified, democratic nation."[42] At the same time in America, the McCarthy witch hunt was gathering force as progressives were harassed and arrested and careers were destroyed.

In Canada, Ottawa used the "red scare" to clamp down on its Chinese citizens. By the early 1950s, the politics of China were a weapon used against the people of Gold Mountain. To hold allegiance to China, or even to speak of it as your ancestral homeland, was tantamount to admitting loyalty to the People's Republic and Communism. As the Korean War developed in 1950, the Chinese in Canada held their breath waiting to see if the conflict would escalate. In the back of their minds, the image of Japanese Canadians uprooted from their families and scattered through ghost towns in British Columbia created terror: when Canada was at war with Japan, Japanese Canadians paid with their community and cultural identity. If China's role in the Korean war were to expand beyond Korea's borders, if Western lives were to be taken by the Chinese, would the people of Gold Mountain be treated any different from the Japanese Canadians?

# Powerless Politics

The politics of China relieved the boredom of dead-end jobs in canneries, laundries and restaurants. It filled the leisure time of bachelor workers, provided valuable trade connections to China for the merchant class, and tapped the hidden reservoir of patriotism for the old country. The tragedy and pathos of the revolutionary drama that climaxed on October 10, 1911, gave the Chinese in Canada a cause for celebration. But all these political events were an ocean away from the stark realities of daily life in a country that wanted Asians only for their muscles or commercial ties. The politics of China kept the people of Gold Mountain in touch with their families and ancestral home, but if a laborer or merchant decided to turn his back on these political ties, he could do so. Not everyone sought refuge in Chinese events; there was a choice between participation or isolation.

The politics of Canada, on the other hand, could not be ignored. Chinese life in Canada was deeply influenced by the thoughts and actions of white Canadians, especially of labor leaders, businessmen, church officials and politicians. These individuals pushed the government of the day to enact laws restricting immigration, the mobility of the Chinese and their families, employment, schooling and military service. In all these matters, the people of Gold Mountain were powerless because they had neither friends in high places nor a powerful government in Peking lobbying on their behalf. Even if they were able to vote—which would have made them equal on paper, at least—they still would be unable to offset their lack of clout in Ottawa.

### The Herd Instinct

Denied the franchise, forced to pay a head tax and restricted by law to certain jobs, many Chinese also faced physical abuse. Young and old were victims of attacks by gangs of youths and bullying mobs. In 1907 it was reported in the Victoria *Times* that young toughs from the Asiatic Exclusion League

> have been congregating at the corner of Herald and Douglas streets and at some point between Chinatown and Rock Bay school and not allowing Chinese pupils to pass them on their way to school.
>
> On several occasions, the lads have been assaulted and in some cases prevented from going to school at all.[1]

Chinese laborers were often driven out of small towns. Between 1898 and 1906, white mobs sprung upon Chinese workers in the Slocan Valley, Atlin, Salmo and Penticton. Mob violence against Chinese was reported as early as the late 1880s in the larger cities, Victoria and Vancouver.[2]

In most cases, Chinese laborers were hired by white bosses in an attempt to control the existing pool of white labor. Pitting Chinese against whites was simply a variation on an old theme. Turning their animosity toward the Chinese, white workers lost sight of the real problems—low wages and unsafe working conditions—and the owners who were responsible for these conditions.

One of the most infamous of these bosses in British Columbia was Robert Dunsmuir (his son James later became premier of the province). Dunsmuir, a rich industrialist who owned vast reserves of coal in mine fields near Nanaimo on Vancouver Island, often used Chinese workers as strikebreakers during the 1880s. In subsequent decades this tactic was repeatedly used by other bosses against white workers, defeating their demands and inflaming their animosity toward the Chinese.

The worst labor conflict revolving around race exploded in August, 1913, when 1,000 angry white workers struck in Nanaimo, virtually seizing control of the town. The mine proprietors dug into their old bag of tricks, hiring Chinese and Japanese workers as strikebreakers. The splitting tactic worked, and propelled the white miners into action. Before long, a contingent of the Vancouver police and a militia unit from Victoria had to be sent in to protect the Asians. The tension in the community was enormous, and the soldiers remained until the outbreak of World War I when the defence of the country took precedence over the protection of Asian and other strikebreakers.[3]

Strikes involving race hatred were facts of life in early labor history. White workers saw Asians as pawns in the hands of the bosses. On their part, Asians were forced to take whatever jobs were offered simply to survive in a country that restricted them from working in most jobs. Sometimes, when the profit picture required it, the bosses called on their friends in the police or military to protect Asian workers. At other times, when these workers were dispensible, they were left to the mercy of the labor market. Many murders took place in the night.

One night in May, 1883, a white mob armed with clubs snuck into a construction camp near Lytton and pounced on the sleeping Chinese workers. Nine were beaten into unconsciousness; the rest fled. By the time the charred ruins of the camp turned cold and the battered bodies of two murdered Chinese laborers were lowered into the ground, the minor argument between the white foreman and a Chinese bookman which had precipitated the killings was forgotten. Victoria did post a $500 reward for information leading to the capture of the assailants,[4] but whites rarely faced trial when the victim was Asian.

It was only a matter of time before an even larger explosion would rock the Chinese community. After years of isolated cases of harassment, assault and even murder against Asians in B.C., the scope of racist violence took a quantum leap on September 7, 1907, when white agitators attacked Vancouver's Chinatown and the Japanese community. Whipped into a frenzy of hatred by speeches from labor, church and Asiatic Exclusion League demagogues, a crowd of about 1,000 left their meeting and headed to the nearby streets of Chinatown. A rock crashed through a window of a Chinese tailor shop. The riot escalated quickly from there. The mob surged through the streets, smashing windows, looting and threatening to assault Chinese merchants. A few blocks away, Japanese shops and businesses were also attacked.[5]

The Chinese barricaded their stores and tried to hide, but the Japanese made a stand against the mob and pushed it back. As suddenly as it began that day, the violence against the Asian people stopped. To prevent further assaults, the Chinese and Japanese, according to the Vancouver *Daily World*,

> were practically standing under arms and both stated openly that there would be bloodshed if any further attempts were made on them by the mob. The Chinese mostly kept indoors with all the lights out in front of the buildings, but the Japanese paraded in front of their houses on Powell Street and had pickets posted at the approaches to the Japanese quarter. These men were all armed with clubs or guns or knives or all three. Revolvers stuck out of hip pockets, sheath knives hung from belts and the least sign of disturbance caused doors to open and more men, armed with axes, to appear.[6]

Although the Japanese reopened their shops for half a day on the following Monday, the Chinese withdrew all services from the public.[7] House servants stayed away from work; restaurants and laundries catering to a white clientele hung out "closed" signs. Chinatown businesses for non-Chinese people ground to a halt. These actions were the only ones the Chinese community could have used to defend against the threat of goons and further riots. Lacking political power or well-placed allies, Gold Mountain people could respond only in an economic way.

Although 24 rioters, out of almost a thousand, were eventually tried and even jailed for a maximum of six months or fined up to $105,[8] other attacks on the Chinese community continued. Laws were passed forbidding the Chinese from hiring white help in any business. In 1912, Saskatchewan's legislative assembly passed an act (later amended to include only the Chinese) making it an offence to:

> employ in any capacity any white woman or girl or permit any white woman or girl to reside or lodge in or to work in or, save as a *bona fide* customer...to frequent any restaurant, laundry or other place of business or amusement owned, kept, or managed by any Japanese, Chinamen or other Oriental person.[9]

In 1914, British Columbia enacted a statute preventing the hiring of white women in businesses owned by "men of certain races, irrespective of nationality."[10]

In Victoria there were also attempts to segregate Chinese pupils from whites because of "the mode of life, customs and characteristics of these Asiatic younglings, which, it is held, tends to lower the surrounding influence of school life."[11] The Chinese community in Victoria reacted with angry denunciations against the bigoted attacks on their children. They enjoyed some success but were unable to prevent the sporadic segregation of classes in the city's school system.

The campaign to establish permanent segregated schools in

Victoria was spearheaded by the municipal inspector, George H. Deane of the Victoria school board. He told the Victoria *Colonist* that "there is a danger in these Chinese boys....We know that there is not only a tendency with the Chinese to live in unsanitary quarters, but a practice."[12] Based on these racist stereotypes, Deane launched a campaign in January, 1922, to relocate the 216 Chinese pupils in one central location by September of the new school year.

His efforts were less than successful. When the new school opened it doors in the fall, the Chinese students were conspicious by their absence. Boycott—the useful tool against racism taken up by Chinese shopkeepers—was now being used by irate Chinese parents as well. Their resistance to the school board's plan arose in part from their desire to have their children learn English. A separate school would widen the gap between the Chinese people and the others and would renew accusations that the Chinese had no desire to adopt English as their working language and, consequently, no desire to integrate into the wider Canadian society.

As parents, the Chinese naturally wanted a say in their children's schooling. As taxpayers, they found the leverage to take effective action. A proposal was made by Chinese parents and merchants of the local CBA to set up an alternative school in Chinatown. School taxes usually sent to the Victoria schools would be reinvested in this Chinese-only school. Since the school board would lose control over this money as well as the destiny of the Chinese children, it caved in. By September, 1923, 207 Chinese pupils had re-enrolled in mixed-race classes.[13]

### The Exclusion Act and the War Years

By the time Chinese children took their place alongside white students, the Canadian government had already passed the Chinese Immigration Act. Before its implementation on July 1, 1923, however, the Chinese had made a concerted effort to block it. In Vancouver, an unwieldly executive group of 24, backed up by a leadership committee of 64, set up eight fund-raising units to help finance the struggle.[14] Given the many and diverse factional interests in Chinatown, such a large body of decision makers was not surprising. But in such a bureaucracy important voices could and would be muffled. Kin and clan ties affecting one executive member but not another could impede the shaping of policy.

Vancouver's ad hoc committee against the exclusion act represented the largest Chinese community in Canada. The committee, however, lacked clout in Ottawa. Recognizing this, members of Toronto's Chinatown set up the Chinese Association of Canada. Claiming leadership of the people of Gold Mountain, it sought to establish chapters from Victoria to Halifax. This action probably set the Vancouver group against joining the association, even though the association could lobby more efficiently. Since members of the CBA belonged to the Vancouver ad hoc committee, and since the CBA itself was national in scope, the establishment of an association with the same country-wide aspirations was certain to be viewed as a direct challenge. If British Columbia was to be represented, it had to have a representative outside of Vancouver. Lau Kwang-Jo (Joseph Hope) of Victoria, therefore, was a compromise candidate from the west coast.[15]

Without Vancouver's support the association's campaign against the exclusion act was doomed. However, even if the Chinese factions had aligned themselves the situation would have been bleak. Even if the Vancouver group bowed to Toronto's leadership—and there was a geographical rationale behind making Toronto the head of the movement—the people of Gold Mountain had neither the money nor well-placed lobbyists to bend the will of politicians.

Despite the barring of Chinese workers from Canada after July, 1923, the Chinese did not cease in their campaign for status as Canadian citizens. In Ottawa, their petitions were often met with indifference or even hostility. Because of their small numbers (less than 1 per cent of the population) Chinese voters would have little impact, positive or negative, on a politician's chances for re-election. Opposition to the Chinese demands must have been based on something more petty than pure self-interest. In any case, the Chinese community did not want to swing elections, wanting only equality with other Canadians—and that meant, among other things, the right to vote.

The Chinese were predictably confused about the meaning of Canadian citizenship. Looking back to the recent war, they recalled the rhetoric which defined service in the armed forces as the mark of the true patriot. For a few hundred second-generation Chinese from Victoria and Vancouver, fighting against German and Austrian soldiers during World War I showed their commitment to Canada. It was not immediately appreciated. Two years after World War I ended, the twelve Chinese veterans who served in Canada's army were given the federal vote (along with 140 Japanese-Canadian soldiers).[16] They could not exercise their right, however, because the Dominion Elections Act passed the same year made voting in provincial elections a precondition to the federal franchise.[17]

About 500 Chinese soldiers served in Canada's army during World War II.[18] The actual number of Chinese Canadians eligible for service was 8,000 but most of these were single men or widowers, born outside Canada and without dependents.[19] Casualties among the Chinese soldiers were light.

Some of those 500 belonged to Chan Dun's family. One of them was Roy, his fifth son, who fought behind Japanese lines in Borneo, where he contacted malaria. Chinese Canadian pilots also volunteered to fight against the Japanese; the Winnipeg *Free Press* reported that several aviators were preparing to go to China:

## ORIENTAL WINGBIRDS
### Winnipeg airmen ready to return
### to mother country when called
Belief that within the next few months every Chinese aviator in Canada and the United States would be ordered to return to the mother country and take up the fight

against Japanese forces, was expressed Thursday evening by Charles Wong, one of Winnipeg's oriental wingbirds.[20]

China, of course, could not and did not order any Chinese Canadians to join the Allied cause. But it would not have had to in any case: the Chinese Canadian community leaders jumped on the war-wagon with enthusiasm. In Calgary, for example, the Anti-Japanese League threatened to expose and ostracize Chinese Canadians opposing the war; those who failed to hear the Allies' call were branded "traitors to the Chinese people." The Chinese consulate in Ottawa offered to keep a list of dissenters, and where they had property in China, said they would have it "sealed off" at the Anti-Japanese League's request.[21]

Chinese Canadians were also exhorted by their leaders to pitch in financially to the Allied cause. Because China was involved, it became a moral as well as patriotic duty to do so. It is not known to what extent Chinese Canadians shared their leaders' enthusiasm for the war, but as Chinese and as Canadians they were doubly pressured, and they, too, became caught up in the fight to save Western democracy and free enterprise.

Because of China's resistance to Japanese aggression, a new, positive image of the Chinese as allies began to blossom in Canada, especially after Pearl Harbor. Now, money sent to China did not provoke the age-old accusation that the Chinese in Canada were sojourners, interested only in China. Actually, cash donations were sent to China from Canada as early as 1937, when the Chinese war with Japan began. That year, the people of Gold Mountain began a bond sale campaign to aid the resistance. A Chinese Liberty Fund Association was set up and the branch in Victoria collected $69,000 between January, 1938, and April, 1939.[22]

The status of Chinese Canadians soared even higher when compared to the Japanese Canadians, the "other" Asians, who were expelled from the west coast in 1942. A series of federal government orders in council starting on February 24, 1942,[23] passed to appease the government's racist political allies on the west coast, forced the removal of the Japanese to British Columbia's interior and parts of Alberta (a policy vigorously approved by Prime Minister King).

The soldiers of Gold Mountain were divided into two training camps. Major-General George R. Pearkes, the general officer overseeing the Pacific Command, ran a clandestine training operation on Okanagan Lake which would house and equip an elite corps of Chinese Canadian commandos drilled on the finer points of demolition, sabotage and reconnaisance. These specially-trained soldiers would put their lives on the line in Japanese-controlled territories.[24] The other Chinese recruits were not segregated but trained alongside the regular troops of the armed forces. For the first time in the history of Canada, Chinese Canadians were treated the same as any other Canadians, at least on paper. Lieutenant-General J.C. Murchie was responsible for the proposal which sought to minimize any differences between the soldiers of Gold Mountain and the others.[25]

The loyalty displayed by the soldiers of Gold Mountain paved the way for the granting of the franchise. By 1947, two groups had been campaigning for the repeal of the exclusion act, and ultimately for the vote. In Vancouver, Foon Sien of the CBA lobbied politicians and other potentially sympathetic men of influence. The most effective group, however, was a Toronto committee which, besides recruiting the usual Chinese leaders, was able to attract the support of a white lawyer concerned with human rights in Canada, top-ranking church people, and organized labor.[26]

White working-class involvement in the campaign of an ethnic people historically viewed as its economic competitors would have been surprising in 1887 or 1907. But this was 1947, and still fresh were memories of World War II in which Chinese Canadian troops proved themselves courageous battlefield compatriots. At home, there was new hope, especially in the economy. Prices and wages rose quickly and the gross national product grew by more than 25 per cent. By

1948, the postwar boom was taking off.[27] It was only when times were severe that the Chinese would be used as scapegoats for Canada's economic ills. These times were not now.

In 1947, labor's endorsement of the civil rights struggle of Chinese Canadians attracted the progressive segment of the white population. Eventually, the predominantly white-supported Committee for the Repeal of the Chinese Immigration Act became the spearhead in persuading parliament to abolish the exclusion act. On the heels of this repeal came the right to vote in provincial and federal elections. Later, Chinese Canadians gained the municipal franchise.[28]

## Decline of the CBA

The CBA, which always claimed to be the voice of the people of Gold Mountain, was unable to mount a sustained national campaign against the introduction of the exclusion act. It failed to play a major role in the movement that ultimately repealed the act and brought the vote to the people of Gold Mountain. This inability to organize was not, however, the result of the CBA's own doing.

The world of Chinese Canada was changing quickly. Chinese communities by 1923, and even more so by 1947, had sprung up across Canada as far east as St. John's, Newfoundland; Victoria and Vancouver were no longer the centre of Chinese life in Canada. Power began to shift eastward with the movement of people. Toronto's Chinatown was fast becoming an economic and, more importantly, political competitor for the position of the leading voice of Chinese Canada. Recognition as the official interpreter of Chinese events to the wider community and to government officials was the plum for which prestige seekers in the Chinese communities vied. If a leading merchant, doctor, dentist or lawyer in Toronto, for example, was considered the spokesperson of Chinatown by city hall or the Ontario government, he could arbitrate in disputes between the Chinese community and the wider world. If his power as an intermediary extended beyond one city and included all of Canada, so vast would be his authority that he could rule like a benevolent Confucian gentry. Because of Toronto's proximity to Ottawa and its location in the industrial heartland of English Canada, Chinese Canadian wealth and expertise began to travel eastward. In some ways, Toronto's Chinatown was able to rally necessary white support because the image of the Asians as an economic rival had less of a hold on the eastern imagination (although when times were bad, this image incited easterners and westerners equally).[29] With the emergence of Toronto as the major force in Chinese Canada, the CBA in Vancouver became outdated and slid into parochialism.

The CBA suffered another blow, ironically, when the Chinese won the right to vote. Ambitious Chinese Canadians could now work toward a legal, medical or other professional career. These professions neither threatened nor helped the CBA directly, but the Chinese social worker on the government payroll gradually made the CBA's welfare programs obsolete. It was not the first blow to the CBA's welfare programs. Some federal money had been available since the depression for welfare assistance, but Chinese laborers suffered more than their white counterparts because racism even determined who received social assistance. Cash or food was not automatic for the destitute colored people of Canada, who in many cases were simply ignored. Sometimes a group of hungry Chinese workers clamored and shouted on the steps of city hall for food. One, Lee Wei, recalled:

We were lucky in Saskatchewan, in Regina. Once a week, the city gave each Chinese ten pounds of rice and a pound of salt pork. Then we went to a Chinese store, bought five or ten cents worth of pickled vegetables, steamed it with some salt and pickled vegetables, cooked a few kernels of rice, ate it, that was it.

If the city didn't give us anything, we'd have starved to death.[30]

As the level of government closest to the people, municipal governments were obliged to be more active in providing relief. After World War II, the federal government became more involved in welfare assistance in an attempt to control potentially dissident individuals. But it was not until the Canada Assistance Plan of 1966 that Ottawa and the provinces consolidated previous cost-sharing programs such as unemployment assistance, old age pension, child welfare, administrative expenses and disabled persons' aid.[31] This effectively ended the CBA's traditional role of helping destitute Chinese workers.

### The New Village People

A 1967 order in council amending the 1952 Immigration Act created an influx of Chinese settlers not only from China but also from such places as Taiwan, Malaysia, Trinidad, Jamaica, India, South Africa, the Philippines and Peru. They brought with them the same hopes and desires as their compatriots had in the nineteenth century. Within two years 8,382 had immigrated to Canada.[32] The amendment to the Immigration Act was essentially non-discriminatory. Theoretically, immigrants were judged on the basis of education, job qualification and experience, and language ability in either English or French. A family-reunion scheme allowed relatives of Canadians to apply under the direct sponsorship of the relative. The amendment was an attempt to quash restrictions on the basis of nationality, ethnic group, class or area of origin. "Peculiar customs, habits, modes of life" as well as "unsuitability having regard to the climatic, economic, social, industrial, educational, health, or other conditions" were considered inconsequential. There was, however, a clause which judged qualification for admission according to the applicant's "probable inability to become readily assimilated or to assume the duties and responsibilities of Canadian citizenship within a reasonable time after admission."[33]

But the amendment was a boon to the Chinese communities across Canada. Chinese immigrants arriving after 1967 invigorated dying or stagnant Chinatowns, especially in the larger cities like Vancouver, Toronto and Montreal. This influx changed the entire composition of Gold Mountain. No longer the self-sufficient, self-generating urban villages isolated by racism from the mainstream of Canadian life and society, Chinatowns took in new ideas, values, dialects and outlooks. They were quickly becoming cosmopolitan villages in the larger urban areas, though they were withering in such places as Lethbridge, Saskatoon and Edmonton. In Vancouver, Toronto and Montreal, Chinatowns could no longer function as narrow urban villages dominated by Confucian values and manners. Only Victoria's Chinatown, because of its remoteness from the rest of Canada and its own long tradition, was able to retain some semblance of these traditional features.

The loss of traditional roles, coupled with the arrival of Chinese immigrants from areas beyond its kin and clan control, left the CBA struggling to survive in a world of change. One of its props, association with the Guomindang, was shaken when Chiang Kai-shek was forced into exile on Taiwan in 1949. Without much legitimacy either in China or Canada's Chinatowns the CBA was a moribund organization until the 1970s.

Canada's recognition of the People's Republic of China in October, 1970, roused the dormant membership of the CBA into action, and it began lobbying on behalf of the Taiwan government.[34] No longer a social force dedicated to providing welfare programs and defending Chinatown residents from racist abuse, the CBA was reborn as a single-issue political organization. Its leader in 1970, Lam Fong, prided himself in his image as the "commissioner of overseas affairs" for Taiwan and the voice of Canada's Guomindang.[35] The CBA's grass-roots origins disappeared behind a propaganda mask.

While the CBA battled the imaginary demons from Peking and agonized over the *fait accompli* of recognition, it ignored the issues in Vancouver's Chinatown which touched the daily lives of its people. There were, however, new forces coming into play in the community. An early test of their effectiveness was about to take place. Planners and real estate developers considered Strathcona, the neighborhood where Chinatown was situated, an eyesore. Under the guise of urban renewal, city council in August, 1971, rezoned one block of Chinatown to make way for a firehall next to a Chinese-language school. Homes were expropriated and destroyed; their occupants promised first choice of public housing. At the same time, city hall tried to bulldoze a freeway through Chinatown. A four-lane road was envisioned as a "logical" step to easing the city's traffic congestion. But the proposed artery would have split Chinatown from its commercial outlets. Both projects were shelved after widespread protest from Chinese merchants, Chinatown groups and residents, and a new organization promoting a Chinese Cultural Centre (CCC).

Well-educated and articulate in the English language, the leaders of the CCC were second- and third-generation professionals, students and entrepreneurs, as well as immigrants of the past decade. Since the centre they were planning to build was in the path of the proposed freeway, these new activists were especially anxious to stop its construction. Their noisy, broad-based demonstration helped persuade civic politicians to drop their plans. This was the first major test of the new activists' support and power.

After the freeway threat had been overturned, new challenges to the proposed centre emerged. The CBA was angered by the community support and high media profile of the centre's leaders, as well as its own absence from the project. Pulling its by-now familiar demon out of its hat, the CBA leaders began spreading rumours in late 1974 that the centre concept was a Communist plot. When this tired tactic failed, the CBA decided to form a counter-group, the Chinese Canadian Activity Centre, which proposed a $1.5-million cultural centre separate from the new activists' project. The Activity Centre then proceeded to apply for a government grant in competition with the CCC's own application (placing Ottawa in the uncomfortable position of having to decide which group actually represented the Chinese community).

To counteract the Activity Centre's tactics, the CCC activists set up the Committee to Democratize the CBA. It accurately depicted the CBA as a propaganda front for the Taiwan government, not an organization concerned with the community welfare. Behind the scenes, the committee looked to the Canadian courts for help. Arguing that the CBA leaders had circumvented their own constitution by holding closed elections for the executive positions, the committee took the CBA to the British Columbia Supreme Court in an effort to force open elections. In the spring of 1978, the CBA was ordered by the court to call open elections. When they were held, the pro-Guomindang elements were easily defeated.[36] The CBA would eventually return to its traditional role of fighting racism and once again provide for the political, social and cultural welfare of Vancouver's Chinese community.

### New People in Metro

Land developers and political parvenu under the influence of Taiwan intruded into the lives of Chinese in other cities as well. In Toronto, where the Chinese population was 62,000 by 1967 and spurted to 70,000 in the next decade (thanks largely to the 1967 amendments to the Immigration Act),[37] a new merchant class sprang up to service the burgeoning community. The abundance of skilled workers, the low crime rate and economic stability attracted a host of entrepreneurs and investors to Chinatown's business area, which was centred on Dundas Street West between University Avenue and Spadina.

Of the five richest Chinese in the city, four came from London (England), Manila, Hong Kong and Taiwan; only one made his fortune as a long-time resident of Canada. With their immense wealth and aggressive investments and expansion, these recently arrived entrepreneurs were seen by many of the older and more established merchants as interlopers, interested only in the profits from Chinatown tourism and industries.[38]

The influx of new wealth and the subsequent new shops and restaurants gave rise to the need for workers in Chinatown.

Luckily for Chinatown's new bosses, large numbers of Chinese laborers from all over the world had immigrated to Canada to escape grinding poverty and lack of opportunities in their former homelands. A large pool of non-English-speaking workers was ready to accept the minimum wage or less and eschew job security and many benefits guaranteed by law. Exploitation of workers in Toronto's Chinatown was common. For example, owners would hire a cook or waiter for a few days or weeks. Just before the worker became eligible for unemployment benefits, he was sacked. The bosses were then able to keep the money earmarked for unemployment insurance and also prevent the fired workers from filing a complaint.[39] As in early Chinese Canada, capital accumulation and profit maximization were still the principle factors in the class relations among Chinese Canadians.

Hotels and garment factories on southeast Spadina owned by non-Chinese entrepreneurs also employed Chinese workers. About 85 per cent of the workers in the "rag trade" were non-English-speaking women. Ninety-nine per cent of the women operated the sewing machines—the lowest-paying job in the trade.

Working conditions were abysmal. The workers typically earned $2.65 to $3 an hour. In addition to the Chinese women, Portuguese, Greeks, South Asians and West Indians also operated the machines or engaged in other garment work. For a coat that retailed for $250, an employer would pay $13 in wages. The situation was ripe for union organization. The bosses, naturally, do their best to retain the status quo. They breed dissent among the workers by exploiting race or ethnic differences. Segregated by race or language in the workplace, the workers have almost no communication with other groups. Thus divided, their demands remain weak and their cohesiveness negligible. As new immigrants, their options are few. Because their workplace is in Chinatown, the only world they have known in Canada, they stay put.[40]

Older organizations such as the Chinese Community Centre of Ontario (CCCO) which relied for power on certain kin and

153

clan ties had little influence with the new immigrants, coming as they did from such diverse places of origin. Like the pre-1978 CBA in Vancouver, the CCCO (it was known as the Chinese Protection Federation until 1945) supported Taiwan, and Canada's recognition of China split Toronto's Chinatown into two ideological camps. Many new settlers, who had enough to contend with merely adjusting to Canada, avoided political issues. The once-powerful CCCO fell into factional disputes and a power struggle which continues today began for control of Chinatown's politics.

In the meantime, a new group of Hong Kong-born, Canadian-educated social service workers and community activists began to make an impact on the people of Chinatown. As professional social workers and community organizers, they gradually replaced the traditional Chinatown associations and their welfare functions. Generally in the pay of the Candian state, these new activists became the link between the Chinese working class and various government departments. Because of their grass-roots connections they were an important cog in the control mechanism used by the government to monitor activities of racial groups in Canada. Like the old merchant class, these activists received suitable rewards for their work. Government connections gave the new professionals a legitimacy and recognition by the state that would allow them to assume leadership of Toronto's Chinese community, and eventually of such communities across the country. Such a position brought with it public recognition and considerable influence—in the matter of allocation of federal multiculturalism grants, to take one example. For many new Chinese immigrants, especially those from British-dominated Hong Kong where social and political recognition depended on skin color, social and political status was highly regarded and sought after. As in Hong Kong, however, it was possible to achieve these ambitions in the Chinese community alone.

Sometimes the new activists striving to become the leaders of the Chinese community gave up their role as activists once the state recognized them as the voice of Chinatown. Those who stayed on, the social workers, professionals, etc., could survive as community leaders only if they supported community interests.

One of the major issues after 1969 was the redevelopment of Toronto's Chinatown. The activists' major proposal to the city's planning department was to retain the character of Chinatown by preventing high rise apartment blocks and restricting commercial buildings to four storeys. The proposition was designed to hinder attempts to rezone the industrial/garment areas of Chinatown, which provided many jobs for Chinese workers.

The new Chinese money had different ideas. They wanted to turn the district into a profitable investment centre. For this, rezoning would be necessary. The new developers proposed a complex of expensive condominiums, unavailable to the average workers but within the grasp of the middle class; office buildings geared toward the new business elite of Chinatown; and boutiques selling chic fashions and accessories. Naturally, such construction would inflate surrounding property values. The developers would profit enormously but the rag trade merchants would find their premises becoming too expensive. Leaving Chinatown with them would be the jobs of the Chinese working class in the area.

The developers allied themselves with the traditional merchant associations such as the pro-Guomindang Chinese Community Centre of Ontario, which saw the coalition as a way of opposing and weakening the influence of the new activists. The old guard would have a chance to recoup their lost status and power in the community.[41]

The leaders of the developers' coalition were pillars of the old Chinatown establishment: a prominant lawyer whose firm represented one of the investment firms; the president of the Chinese Businessman's Association, a sort of local chamber of commerce; and another Chinatown businessman and politician who represented the ward on city council.[42] They stressed the economic benefits their plan would bring to the community. The activists for their part expressed the fear that if Chinatown changed to suit the developers' interests, Chinese workers would lose their jobs so that a few investors could profit. They also emphasized the elitist composition of the entrepreneurial alliance, while asserting their own diverse origins and ethnic representation. After wrangling that spanned many months, Toronto's city council came down on the side of the developers. They were at least partly swayed by the support for the proposals expressed by the aforementioned Chinatown alderman, perceived by many in the white community to accurately reflect the interests of a Chinese community they did not understand. It appears that the landscape of Toronto's Chinatown will change forever in the 1980s.

The struggle over development of the Chinatowns in Toronto and Vancouver saw new versions of the old Chinese classes arise. The merchant/gentry became the developer/investor, and the poor laborer or peasant became the working class. But while China's impoverished classes were poorly represented, this new working class was developing its own articulate, well-educated leadership.

Christianized Chinese merchants, Vancouver, 1920s

The Celestial Gents, 1940s

國 民 捐 獎 狀

為發給獎狀事案查國務院議決修正國民捐
獎勵章程第一條第七項募得自一千元以上
有捐至一百元以下者由財政部總長贈與獎
狀等因協查有城多利卑
陳藝先生自捐　　拾　　元　　角合行
查照該章程第一條第七項由本總長給與
獎狀以資執守丙昭激勵頒至獎狀者

右致

陳藝先生收執

財政總長熊希齡

中華民國二年十二月三十一日

域宇第壹千伍百伍拾陸號

Chan Dun's donation to the Republican cause,
December 31, 1913

Chan Dun's family poses around one of his
flying machines, 1917

158

Koo Shee and Chan Dun proudly flank their fighting sons, Ira, Paul and Roy

The Edmonton protest march against *W5*, January 26, 1980

An anti-*W5* poster

# FOOL'S GOLD

On September 30, 1979, the CTV television network's *W5* public affairs program aired a segment called "Campus Giveaway" which was to become the focus of political activity that would shake the Chinese community for the next two years. The program's blatant racism sparked a degree of public wrath unprecedented in Canada's Chinatowns. On one level the anti-*W5* movement was a response to an attack on Chinese Canadians' rights, but it was also the product of a decade of social protest in the Chinese communities of North America and Hong Kong.

In 1968 and 1969, Asian American students at San Francisco State College and the University of California at Berkeley joined blacks and Chicanos in establishing the so-called Third World strike contingents. This marked the beginning of a new Asian American consciousness and resulted in an increase in political awareness and participation by Asians in American politics (for example, they became vocal opponents of the Vietnam war), the introduction of courses in Asian American culture at United States colleges and universities, and the birth of a body of literature describing the Asian experience in America (Frank Chin and Maxine Hong Kingston are the best-known writers of this genre). It was only a matter of time before the youth in Canada's west coast Chinese communities were infected and began their own search for roots and to formulate a new destiny for themselves in Canada. They developed a new understanding of what it meant to be Chinese in Canada. No longer content to be hyphenated Canadians, the young Chinese became aware of a Chinese tradition in Canada that began with the first fortune seekers of Gold Mountain and had little to do with China. The discovery that their roots lay in Canada, not in China, would be reflected in their writing and music.

Largely because of its proximity to the growing Chinese American literary scene in San Francisco, Vancouver became Chinese Canada's cultural capital.[1]

But the political centre of Chinese activities in Canada was Toronto. The city's Chinese population had grown to about 80,000 by the end of the 1970s, rivalling Vancouver's population of 90,000. In addition to the traditional core of Chinatown on Dundas and Bay Streets and on Spadina Avenue, new Chinese communities sprang up in the Broadview/Gerrard and Agincourt areas. The influx of Chinese immigrants and the "urban renewal" of the inner city Chinatowns by developers forced many Chinese families to move to new locations on the fringes of Toronto.

The increase of non-white immigration into Toronto during the 1970s led to increased racism and harassment of immigrants. Tales of a non-white immigrant pushed off a Toronto subway platform, of "Paki-bashing," and of police raids on black homes hit the newspapers. Although the racial abuse was directed at South Asians more than themselves, some highly conscious Chinese and Japanese began to form campaigns against racism and discrimination.

One of these groups was the Asianadian Resource Workshop, founded in 1978. (One of its organizers, Cheuk Kwan, would play an important role in the anti-*W5* campaign.) The Workshop established links with virtually every other progressive Asian organization in Toronto. While the Workshop never had more than 30 active members at any time, it gained a reputation as a vigilant, sometimes strident, opponent of racism and discrimination.

The Workshop was instrumental in organizing forums on racism in the Asian and non-Asian communities. The *Asianadian*, the Workshop's magazine, featured Asian political movements in Canada, Asians in Quebec, Asian Canadian literature, and the Asian gay rights movement.

The basic principles of the Workshop and its magazine were spelled out in the first issue: "The *Asianadian* will continue to speak out against those factors (whether conditions or persons) perpetuating racism in Canada. It will stand up against the distortions of our history in Canada, stereotypes, economic exploitation, and the general tendency towards injustice and inequality practiced on 'visible minorities.' "[2] The *W5* issue was a natural rallying cry for the Asianadian Resource Workshop.

Another political group in Toronto, progressives who were predominantly social workers raised in the exploitative atmosphere of Hong Kong, championed the rights of new Asian immigrants, mostly garment workers. Many of these activists had taken part in the Hong Kong student demonstrations of 1971 in support of China's claims against Japan for the nearby island of Diao Yutai. The protests resulted in closer police scrutiny of these new, organized activists. During the early 1970s the police were preoccupied with defusing the growing student agitation to have Chinese recognized as one of the two official languages of Hong Kong, which is overwhelmingly Chinese. The British authorities considered this and other protest acts of rebellion and responded accordingly. But they were unable to crush the courageous new movement, which had been influenced by the Cultural Revolution in China and the international student movement sweeping the world in the 1960s.[3] In the eyes of the Hong Kong government officials, the troublemakers were the social workers—many of them working class university or college graduates.[4] Those who remained in Hong Kong continued to agitate. Those who immigrated to Canada brought with them their belief in democratic principles and equality.

The anti-W5 movement in Canada, therefore, was a culmination of the aspirations of disparate but principled men and women seeking changes in the status quo. All of them had been exposed to a wide spectrum of new ideas generated in the late 1960s and 1970s. They and their ancestors had come to Canada because it seemed a land of freedom and equal opportunity, a country that embodied their democratic and professional aspirations. But "Campus Giveaway" mocked their hard work and sacrifices, telling Chinese Canadians they were "foreigners" with no place in Canadian society.

For third generation Canadians, whose roots went back to the gold rush days of the 1850s, the show was a slap in the face. The mines their ancestors had blasted, the railway track they laid, the lives they had lost on the battlefields of war and industry—those contributions seemed to lose all meaning. More than a century of history in Canada had not bleached away Chinese Canadians' "foreign" appearance.

What made many Chinese appear alien, what exemplified their "Chineseness,"[5] was their adherence to Confucianism and its traditions of family and patriarchy. There was also the pressure to excel in school so that their lives could be materially better than those of their parents. In Confucian China as well as democratic Canada, education could wipe out generations of poverty and bestow esteem and status.

"Achievement by merit" was a Confucian principle that every Chinese, whether in China or Canada, learned very young. In every peasant worker home, homilies were handed down from one generation to the next about a poor boy excelling in school, passing the examinations, and becoming a rich and powerful official and landlord.

Education was the way out of poverty and hunger in Imperial China. Rebellion and revolution came and the Chinese monarchy disappeared, but the Confucian idea that education and upward mobility were synonymous held fast, especially in the British colony of Hong Kong, where Confucianism was used to control a potentially rebellious Chinese majority.

Immigrants from Hong Kong and the children of Gold Mountain saw "Campus Giveaway" as a direct threat to their traditional belief in "advancement by merit." To make matters worse, Canadian society too fostered belief in the necessity of education as a stepping stone to material wealth and social success. Because traditional Chinese society and present day Canadian norms upheld the notion of education opportunities, the Chinese were simply pursuing their education in harmony with two value systems.[6] If they could be blamed for anything, it was their simple and naive belief in the principles of Canadian democracy.

## The Great Canadian Con Job

"Campus Giveaway" portrayed the Chinese as alien, unassimilable, insular and competitive. As the camera panned across the faces of students of Chinese ancestry, the show charged that 100,000 foreign students had descended on Canada's campuses, squeezing white Canadian students out of places in the professional schools.

CTV's message was plain—the Chinese were foreigners, regardless of their birthplace. Reminiscent of the charges against early Chinese laborers, the students were accused of coming to Canada to milk the country of its wealth and resources. After using Canada's educational facilities, these "foreigners" would flee to China and Hong Kong with professional degrees financed by the Canadian taxpayer. The Chinese were yet again pictured as transient, as exploiter, as sojourner.[7] The opening remarks of *W5* host Helen Hutchinson conveyed a message of a new Chinese threat:

Here is a scenario that would make a great many people in this country angry and resentful. Suppose your son or daughter wanted to be an engineer, or a doctor, or a pharmacist. Suppose he had high marks in high school, and that you could pay the tuition—but he still couldn't get into university in his chosen courses because a foreign student was taking his place. Well, that is exactly what is happening in this country.[8]

The opening statement was a deliberate attempt to incite mistrust and hostility towards "foreigners." With the camera focused on Chinese faces, there was no doubt to whom Hutchinson was referring.

To back up its allegations, *W5* stated that 100,000 foreign students were crowding Canadian universities.[9] The actual number of foreign students in Canada was "55,000, at all levels of education, including only 20,000 in full-time university studies."[10]

Another statistical distortion centred around Barbara Allan, the heroine of "Campus Giveaway." Using her bitterness to inspire audience sympathy, Allan was portrayed as an aspiring pharmacist who was rejected by the faculty of pharmacy at the University of Toronto because a foreign student had taken her place:

Barbara Allan has been working on and off in her father's St. Catharines, Ontario, pharmacy since she was 12. She graduated from high school with 79.5 per cent. Good marks, but not high enough to get into pharmacy at University of Toronto. When Barbara saw the pharmacy class, she couldn't believe it.

Although only 165 of a thousand applicants qualify, students from overseas make up 10 to 30 per cent of the class.[11]

While Helen Hutchinson narrated Allan's emotional outcry against foreign students, CTV's cameras roamed the classroom searching out Chinese faces. It isolated six Chinese students: Steven Ng, Teresa Chu, Doris Ng, Faye Wong, Betty Cheung and Jennifer Lee.[12] Jennifer Lee was born in Canada, and the rest were citizens, thus eligible for admission to the pharmacy program. The pharmacy faculty admits Ontario residents only; visa or foreign students are barred.[13]

Barbara Allan was also eligible for admission to the professional school. According to Dr. E.W. Stied, the associate dean of pharmacy: "If she had had the marks she said she did, she would have been accepted. But, according to our records she didn't have those marks."[14] Not having those marks did not prevent Allan from lashing out at the students with "foreign-looking" faces:

> All these people are in, and you're just—you're knocked out of a seat. You are not getting the education that you feel you should be, because it's just—the classes are packed with foreign students.[15]

Yet, few viewers knew the facts. To them, Barbara Allan appeared as the victim of a yellow horde taking her "rightful" place in the university. The emotional impact of "Campus Giveaway" struck at the hearts of the white audience who could sympathize with Allan, a young woman in anguish because her ambitions were snuffed out by the villainous foreign (read "Chinese") students.

### A Community in Protest

At the heart of "Campus Giveaway" was the allegation that foreign students were taking the places of white Canadians in job-directed programs such as pharmacy, computer science, engineering and medicine. Since the foreign faces in the report were Chinese, W5's implication was that all students of Chinese origin were foreigners, and that Canadian taxpayers were subsidizing Chinese students—who would never be truly Canadian, regardless of their birth or citizenship.[16]

Initial reaction to the show in Chinese communities across Canada was subdued. The workers in the Chinatowns and the professionals in the suburbs were preoccupied with their own lives. Some Chinese even missed the allegations of a few vocal students that the program was racist in tone and effect.

While Chinatown and suburbia slept, these students—both Canadian and foreign—bombarded the CTV with protest letters. Forming small study groups, the students initiated a publicity campaign to enlist wider community support. They also sought legal advice to determine whether CTV had libelled and slandered Chinese Canadians. By the end of October the university community in Toronto gradually became aware of the *W5* program, but support from the Chinese community at large was still missing.

### The Student Spark

By November, the apathy among Chinese about the *W5* issue had changed to support and sympathy. This transformation was spearheaded by the students themselves, led by Norman Kwan. Capitalizing on the annual conference of the Council of Chinese Canadians in Ontario (CCCO), the students aired their grievances at the gathering, intended for Chinese community workers, academics, professionals and aspiring politicians. They were informed that an explosive media issue was brewing. The students gave the CCCO delegates an issue and a reason to stand up for their convictions.

The traditional representatives and leaders of the Chinese community, who had gained a high profile because of their business or political connections, shied away from the *W5* controversy. Believing that the students' talk of a libel suit would upset the status quo and endanger their own personal interests, they dismissed the students' grievances as the fulminations of a radical group. While some established figures in the Chinese community did initially participate in the meetings, personal expediency and political ambitions forced them to opt out after only four meetings. As a result, their calls for racial equality and civil rights have since been ineffectual.

Preserving the status quo was not in the interests of the new group of professionals now gaining prominence in the Chinese community. One of these was a physician named Donald Chu. Later to become the chairperson of the Toronto chapter of the anti-W5 movement, Chu was driven to attack W5 because of his "belief in equal rights for all Canadians."[17] Part of the progressive element of the Chinese Canadian intelligentsia that was schooled in Canada, Chu and others rallied firmly behind the students, taking part in an anti-W5 committee.[18] At the heart of the committee, named the Ad Hoc Committee of the CCCO Against W5, was a group of action-oriented people who believed in the Chinese community as a productive and useful contributor to Canadian culture rather than as an object of political and commercial exploitation.

Represented on the Ad Hoc Committee were the Association of Chinese Canadian Students and Graduates, Chinese Canadians for Mutual Advancement, Action Committee for Refugees in Southeast Asia (ACRSEA), Asianadian Resource Workshop and the CCCO. While the students' proposal to sue CTV for libel and slander initially preoccupied the committee, attention also focused on recruiting volunteers to spread the W5 issue throughout the Chinese community. ACRSEA was especially important in the development of a volunteer organization that would provide the human resources for the Ad Hoc Committee.

A community organization based in Toronto's Chinatown, ACRSEA made a tremendous impact with its "Operation Lifeline" project. Dedicated to helping Southeast Asian refugees establish themselves in Canada, ACRSEA gained a reputation for community service. Many of the volunteers who gained experience in the project transferred their community concerns to the political arena and the anti-W5 movement. These men and women formed the backbone of the Toronto chapter. At any given time between November 22, 1979, and April 18, 1980, there were more than 600 volunteers talking up the W5 issue and raising money for the legal and organizational expenses.[19]

Ad Hoc Committee workers distributed pamphlets and leaflets and spoke to church gatherings, social groups, community forums and political rallies throughout the Toronto area. They wrote letters to politicians, ministers and newspapers, and sent representatives to show a tape of "Campus Giveaway" to influential people in various positions of power.

### Street Tactics

By the second week in December, the campaign had yielded only meagre results. The Ad Hoc Committee decided to try a different approach. The protest of ink on paper now gave way to the tactics of direct confrontation—street demonstrations and picketing. This tactic, adopted after a heated meeting in the basement of the Mon Sheung Foundation[20] building (a home for elderly Chinese), aroused considerable opposition by a group later known as the "Professional Four."

Consisting of a lawyer, doctor, dentist and engineer, the Professional Four opposed the "radical" nature of the planned demonstrations and legal action. They also feared the repercussions of supporting the stance of the students. The group believed that a backlash against the Chinese community was almost inevitable if picketing and a legal suit became the Ad Hoc Committee's prime tactics. But a majority of the members held firm and on December 17, a vote of 9-4 carried the day for demonstration and legal action. As one of the committee members said: "We are simply exercising our rights in a democratic Canada."

The question of legal action had already been investigated by the students. Having called on the expertise of a Toronto lawyer with an impressive civil rights record, the students told the committee that a lawsuit could be successful.[21]

To support the lawyer's opinion, Cheuk Kwan, the Ad Hoc Committee's treasurer, brought up a Toronto *Globe and Mail* report of the same week describing a court battle between a South Asian mathematics professor and Seneca College.[22] The professor had accused the college of not hiring her because of her race. The court's verdict—unprecedented in human rights cases in Canada—ruled in favor of granting her monetary compensation.

This case, and the lawyer's recommendation, turned the tide in the crucial legal vote. But the vote split the committee into two opposing camps. Fortunately for the committee, the "Professional Four" bowed out before the split could blossom into destructive bickering. With the strengthened sense of unity, the question of legal action and peaceful demonstrations and picketing gave way to planning and co-ordination.

One of the "Professional Four" was a prominent Eurasian dentist with political ambitions who actually promoted his association with the Ad Hoc Committee Against W5 in his official campaign literature during the 1980 Toronto civic election. But his claim that he was a founding member as well as the initial spokesperson for the group was false. The dentist was not only opposed to legal action but, according to an Ad Hoc representative, "tried to wreck the committee" by calling on the CCCO board of directors on January 7, 1980, to dissolve the Ad Hoc Committee.[23] Yet in his political campaign the dentist tried to portray himself as a civil rights leader defending the rights of Chinese Canadians.

### The Cecil Meeting

On December 19, a rally at the Cecil Community Centre revealed that the W5 issue had united the Chinese community regardless of occupation and political persuasion. The auditorium was filled to capacity for a screening of "Campus Giveaway." Matrons in black silk jackets, ambitious young lawyers, CBA members, aging bachelors from a forgotten era, fashionably dressed students, and small children clutching their parents' hands crammed into the 200 seats and lined the walls. From every corner of the Toronto Chinese community, the W5 issue had brought out the previously uncommitted, apathetic and the sceptical. The atmosphere was electric with the anticipation of momentous developments.

The Cecil meeting demonstrated the depth of the community's feelings about the Ad Hoc Committee's campaign. Many began to believe that a united community dedicated to achieving clear-cut goals could be victorious.

At its first meeting, the Ad Hoc Committee set three objectives:

> • to demand a public apology from CTV and an equal opportunity to present a fair and accurate report to repair the damages done by the W5 program;
> • to take the necessary steps to ensure that CTV does not air similar programs misrepresenting and damaging the image of any ethno-cultural group;
> • to educate the public about the contributions of the Chinese Canadians to Canadian society.[24]

The Cecil turnout convinced the Ad Hoc Committee to stage a peaceful demonstration in Toronto, the media heartland of the country. The plan was to hold a mass rally on January 26, 1980, in the education building on the University of Toronto campus, then march on the CTV headquarters about a mile away.

## "Freedom is Won in Struggle"

The federal election then impending helped attract twenty speakers representing all political parties to the rally. Ron Atkey, the incumbent minister of employment and immigration, did not show but his surrogate told the crowd of 1,000 which packed the auditorium that W5 "was unfair to the extreme" because "the majority of the foreign students came from Europe and the USSR."[25]

Politicians Bob Kaplan, Bob Rae, Peter Stollery, John Foster and Eric Jackson denounced the CTV program. Rae, at that time the NDP MP for the largely Chinese riding of Broadview-Greenwood, said: "The assumption from W5 is that to be white is to be Canadian. And that to be non-white is to be a foreigner. What we must understand is that an immigrant is not a foreigner. As Canadians, we are all boat people."[26]

John Sewell, the mayor of Toronto whose championing of progressive and unpopular causes would lead to his defeat in the next election, called for police and media reform "if we are to create a country where we all feel at home."[27] He blasted the CTV program as "a serious insult to the educational aspirations of Canadians who are not white."[28]

Wilson Head, president of the National Black Coalition, told the predominantly Chinese audience that "CTV did you a favor in arousing in you a need to fight back." It "has incited the Chinese to fight back and face the fact that there is a good deal of bigotry. No one gives you freedom. It is won in struggle."[29]

George Bancroft, an education professor, got the most enthusiastic response when he said: "At the University of Toronto we give grades ranging through A, B, C, D and F for failure. But I would not give *W5* an A, B, C, D or F. I would give it a P...I mean P for pollution in its facts. I mean pollution in analysis. Pollution must be cleaned up. *W5*'s pollution must be removed! Its pollution must be eradicated." When he sat down, the usually subdued Chinese Canadians gave him a deafening ovation.[30]


### "Biased Show, W5 Got to Go"

The roused audience, inspired by these speeches, emptied into the street, where they were met by about 1,500 more protesters. Pickets were unveiled and slogans echoed in the bitterly cold air:

> CTV Apologize Now!
> Red, Brown, Black, Yellow, and White—We Canadians
>     Must Unite
> Biased Show, *W5* Got To Go!

Marching four abreast, the demonstrators headed for the

CTV's national headquarters. The crowd was mostly Chinese, but people from many other ethnic groups in Toronto were there to lend support. Here was multiculturalism in action—ethnic people defending the rights of all Canadians.

Leading the demonstrators were Ad Hoc Committee leaders Donald Chu, Cheuk Kwan and Joseph Wong. In front of the CTV office, Chu told the protesters that the W5 program "encourages stereotyping and discrimination of a multicultural society under the guise of freedom of speech. It is irresponsible journalism that must be suppressed. We need all Canadians to support the cause and promote mutual understanding." He later told reporters that "we'll keep up the pressure through all avenues...by peaceful means, of course."[31]

Cheuk Kwan delivered a letter of protest intended for CTV president Murray Chercover. Chercover, however, had chosen not to meet with the demonstrators and instead sent Lionel Lumb, the producer of "Campus Giveaway," to meet with reporters but not with the Ad Hoc Committee's representatives. In a prepared statement, Lumb said, "As producer of W5, I strongly disagree with the position taken by today's protesters. But in view of the fact that certain parties have chosen the courts to judge the veracity and accuracy of the statements contained in W5's campus story, I cannot comment further because that might prejudice CTV's case before the courts."[32]

When the demonstration ended, one 70-year-old Chinese said, "I have been here for 56 years and I am very happy that at last we have the courage to stand up." Busloads of supporters from Hamilton, Windsor, Ottawa and Montreal had also joined the Toronto rally; in all, more than 160 organizations representing every ethnic group in Canada took up placards against the CTV.

### A Single Spark
Toronto was not the only scene of picketing and protest against CTV. On the same day, more than 500 demonstrators marched in the bitter cold on CTV's Edmonton affiliate, CFRN.

174

The protest, led by the Ad Hoc Committee of Chinese Canadians in Edmonton Against *W5*, which had been formed in early January after a member of the Toronto Ad Hoc Committee had brought the issue of "Campus Giveaway" to Edmonton's Chinese community, was supported by groups from Calgary and Vancouver. The marchers delivered a letter of protest to CFRN station manager Bruce Alloway. Alloway's response was the same as Lionel Lumb's: he refused to make any statement because it would "be inappropriate while legal action initiated by the Chinese community in Toronto was underway."[33]

The Edmonton protest showed that the anti-*W5* movement had spread beyond Canada's "heartland," but the Toronto rally was the centrepiece in the movement. Publicized across Canada, its success heightened the Toronto Ad Hoc Committee's realization that only a national movement could persuade the CTV to apologize.

Through friendship, school and kinship ties, Toronto had established lines with Montreal, Vancouver, Edmonton, Calgary and Saskatoon before January 26. But the task in the post-rally days was to form Ad Hoc Committees in all the remaining major cities where the CTV operated. Ad Hoc Committees were formed in Winnipeg, Regina, Vancouver, Edmonton, Calgary and Saskatoon at the initiative of the Toronto organizers. The only committee in the Maritimes, the Nova Scotia Chinese Ad Hoc Committee Against *W5*, was formed spontaneously without direction from Toronto but became part of the national organization on March 14, 1980.[34] By the time CTV responded on March 16 to the public outcry against "Campus Giveaway," sixteen active Ad Hoc Committees were in operation from Victoria to Halifax. This type of social movement was unprecedented in Chinese Canadian history. The Chinese community, once stereotyped as passive and docile, was now action-oriented and conscious of its own democratic rights.

## Negotiations

Although the Toronto demonstrators had been given a curt response by Lionel Lumb, CTV was disturbed by the unfavorable publicity generated by the Chinese community across Canada, and requested a meeting. Held on February 4 and attended by Donald Chu and Joseph Wong of the Toronto committee and the network's vice president and executive producer Don Cameron and Lionel Lumb, the meeting produced nothing concrete. The committee reiterated its demands: a public apology, a fair and accurate program to repair the damage done and a promise not to air other programs that might damage the image of any ethno-cultural group.[35]

On February 11, the Toronto committee and the five student plaintiffs hired lawyer Ian Scott as their negotiator. The Ad Hoc Committee's decision to use a lawyer was a reminder to the CTV that legal action was imminent if the network did not negotiate sincerely and seriously.

Four days later, the Ad Hoc Committee sent Cheuk Kwan to appear before Toronto's city council in an effort to exert further pressure on CTV. The council passed a motion by Ying Hope, the alderman for the predominantly Chinese ward of Spadina, condemning the irresponsible journalism of CTV in its *W5* "Campus Giveaway" program. The council also issued a formal complaint to the Canadian Radio-Television and Tele-communications Commission (the federal agency regulating broadcasting) about *W5* and asked for public hearings on the issue.[36]

## The Non-Apology

While the Ad Hoc Committees across Canada filed complaints to provincial and federal human rights bodies and amassed 20,000 signatures on a petition protesting the *W5* program,[37] CTV tried to diffuse the movement by issuing a statement of "regret." On March 16, Helen Hutchinson said on *W5* that the earlier show had "upset two groups of Canadians:

176

the universities, who said the facts were inaccurate, and the Chinese Canadian community, who said the program was racist and cast slurs upon its members.... W5 would like to say this: it was never our intention in doing the program to give offence to *any* Canadian community: W5 sincerely regrets any offence that may have been unintentionally given to the Chinese Canadian community."[38]

CTV's expression of "regret" was not, however, any apology. The statement tried to blame the Ad Hoc Committee for the stalemate preventing resolution of the issue. Because the program "upset the universities and the Chinese Canadian community," Hutchinson said, "W5 last November began preparing a follow-up program in which we intended to invite the Chinese Canadian community to present its point of view. But soon after, a libel suit was brought against W5 by some individuals, and our legal advice prevented us from airing the second program. W5 six weeks ago...on its own initiative sought a meeting with the Ad Hoc Committee of the Council of Chinese Canadians Against W5. At the meeting, W5 voluntarily offered to seek ways of resolving the situation. W5 is still waiting to hear back from the committee."[39]

The March 16 statement set off a national reaction among the Ad Hoc Committees. The Vancouver local committee asserted that CTV's "regret" was "wholly inadequate to redress the damage done by the story to the Chinese Canadian community."[40] It pointed out that the Chinese Canadians and the university community were not the only groups upset by the program. "Labor unions, educational groups and a diversity of social and ethnic organizations have issued statements against the story." The major problem with the CTV statement, the Vancouver group continued, was that "no fault is admitted other than the admission that one of the statistics quoted in the story was in error, and even the admission is qualified. The impression thus created by the statement is that the Chinese Canadian community has launched a deep and vociferous nation-wide protest over a single statistical error. This is in itself condescending and

177

insulting to all the many good Canadians who have joined the protest. The error admitted was only one of the many faults of the story and it was far from the worst."

The Vancouver committee concluded that "the reasons for the protest are not acknowledged but rather ignored. The issues raised are studiously evaded. There is no indication in the statement that *W5* really understands what was wrong with the story in the first place."[41]

In Edmonton, Patrick Ma, vice-president of the Ad Hoc Committee there, said CTV made "no mention of the mistakes they made in calling all orientals 'foreigners,' which is our prime concern."[42] This grievance was also repeated by the Toronto committee, which labelled the March 16 statement a "white-wash."[43] Summing up the conflict, Donald Chu said that the CTV "did not address the most important issue—that the Chinese Canadians were being cast as foreigners in the program 'Campus Giveaway.'"

"The Ad Hoc Committee was surprised to learn that it was to participate in a follow-up program," he continued. "At no time had the committee been approached by CTV or *W5* to participate in such a program." The real problem was "that *W5* simply chose to dismiss the nature of the complaints, and that the nature of the complaints about the program has not been absorbed by CTV."[44]

Siukeong Lee of the Montreal Ad Hoc Committee angrily replied that "after clearly insulting all Chinese Canadians, CTV now wants to walk away by gently regretting the offence that may have been given and says it is unintentional. We say this is neither honest nor fair. CTV must face the issue, admit all mistakes, apologize, and compensate."[45]

In Halifax, the Nova Scotia Ad Hoc Committee said that CTV's statement "is not being taken as an apology." The network "did not fully own up to the racism and inaccuracies inherent in the program and did not recognize the protests which have been waged against it." What CTV was attempting to do was to undercut the movement. But this "only adds fuel to the flame of what *W5* is doing."[46]

CTV's response to the latest outcry was conveyed by Lionel Lumb. "The statement was made in a positive way," he said. "I don't understand these complaints. The statement expressed sincere regret." According to Lumb, the statement "was the equivalent of putting a retraction on the front page of a newspaper." He added that "we didn't bury it. We said it right up front where we have the majority of the viewers." He denied that the purpose of the statement was to diffuse anger.

After receiving CTV's lame reply, the Toronto Ad Hoc Committee announced that "CTV is not likely to accept our demands voluntarily" because "if CTV admits that it has made a major mistake, it stands to lose its credibility. Therefore, not only is CTV not going to accede to our demands voluntarily, it is going to stage a long and hard resistance to delay the inevitable." In doing so, "CTV can hope to achieve two goals: first, it may be able to avoid apologize only after the issue and our grievances are long forgotten by the public, thus doing minimal damage to its credibility and at the same time remedying very little of the damage it did to the Chinese Canadian community."[47]

The Toronto Ad Hoc Committee decided to mount a sustained campaign against CTV and called together the fifteen committees across the country for a meeting in Toronto. The strategy behind this gathering was to demonstrate to CTV that the anti-*W5* movement embraced Chinese communities throughout Canada.

While plans were going ahead for the April 18 to 20 national meeting, CTV and the Toronto Ad Hoc Committee met on April 3. Lawyer Scott restated the Ad Hoc Committee demands and called on the CTV to negotiate. At this meeting, CTV finally realized the extent of the anger of the Chinese over being labelled "foreigners" in "Campus Giveaway," and that inaccurate statistics were not the major issue. On April 15, the CTV and the Ad Hoc Committee agreed on a settlement package. The next day, CTV issued a public apology. The network's top executive, Murray Chercover, said that "Campus Giveaway" "was largely based on extrapolations that distorted the actual statistics...the majority of the research data was incorrect. We were clearly wrong in our presentation of the facts and *W5*'s initial defence of the program."

The program, Chercover continued, "was criticized by Chinese Canadians and the universities as racist. They were right..." He confessed that "there is no doubt that the distorted statistics combined with our visual presentation, made the program appear racist in tone and effect. We share the dismay of our critics that this occurred. We sincerely apologize for the fact Chinese Canadians were depicted as foreigners, and for whatever distress this stereotyping may have caused them in the context of our multicultural society."

Finally, Chercover said that "corrective measures have been taken. We believe we have now instituted a better system of checks and balances in respect to editorial control and presentation of programs."[48] Marge Anthony, CTV's public relations director, told reporters after the apology that the person chiefly responsible for the "distortions" in the segment "is no longer with us."[49] CTV's internal justice system brought this nasty episode to a close by reporting on October 17, 1980, that Lionel Lumb had quit. Asked about the resignation, Lumb's boss Don Cameron said, "That was just between him and me. That was an internal thing. You know, people quit."[50]

### Chinese Canadian National Council for Equality

The anti-*W5* movement did not disappear with CTV's apology, but evolved into the Chinese Canadian National Council for Equality, a Toronto-based organization to "safeguard the dignity and equality of all Chinese Canadians and other ethnic groups in this country."[51]

The CCNCE was the next logical step in the evolution of the Ad Hoc Committees; a national organization had to be established. The members knew that the struggle for equality and justice did not end with Chercover's apology.

The CCNCE was founded at a three-day conference in April, 1981, at the University of Toronto. While the delegates (most of them men) debated for two days the proposed objectives and structure of the new civil rights organization, the key issue was not the question of racism, but sexism against Chinese women.

At the heart of this issue was the sometimes-heated discussion over the inclusion of a women's secretariat to "identify practices, traditions, assumptions and stereotypes of racial and sexual discrimination against Chinese women." Providing special assistance to Chinese women to achieve equality in the home, workplace and school, the secretariat "would develop and co-ordinate affirmative action program for Chinese women."[52]

Unfortunately, the proposal was not taken seriously by most delegates. A skeletal office was eventually set up as simply a token gesture, prompting one delegate to say that "Chinese Canadians may not have fully realized the meaning of institutional racism (not personal, not in terms of intent, but in terms of effect or impact); thus they were not quite aware of the existence of sexism in our society, or the fact that racism and sexism are closely related. The position of the Chinese woman in Canada must be more carefully examined."[53]


### Blueprint for Victory

There were two major reasons for the success of the anti-*W5* movement. One, few of its volunteers lived or had a business in Chinatown, and could not be accused of using Chinatown for personal gains. The second reason was the physical presence of the anti-*W5* workers in Toronto's Chinese community. They were on the streets of Chinatown even in the dead of winter spreading publicity, soliciting donations and holding fund-raising dances, variety shows and public forums. The movement's presence in the community was beyond dispute.

On top of these activities, the Ad Hoc Committees across Canada looked to the churches, government agencies, media and private groups for support.[54] For the first time in Canadian history, the Chinese actively went outside their communities and into the mainstream of Canadian society in search of allies.

"Justice was done," said Donald Chu, "not because of our efforts alone; the decency, fairness and compassion of many Canadians also contributed to our success."[55]

The glue that held the different groups together, however, was "Campus Giveaway" itself. The program was clearly wrong and racist, it provided an issue that was morally unequivocal. Most Ad Hoc Committee members were native or naturalized Canadians or permanent residents of Canada. "Campus Giveaway" had made them realize that they were still "foreigners"—despite their Canadian jobs, experience, education and life style.

For the Chinese who scrimped, who lived in basement suites and spent endless hours studying to finish their professional degrees, their sacrifices meant little if, at the end of it all, they were still aliens in Gold Mountain. Protest was the only feasible response.

### Failure

On December 1, 1980, *W5* offered its reparation to Chinese Canadians in the form of a fourteen-minute segment called "White and Bright." Showing a day in the life of the Canadian Civil Liberties Association, it exposed racism in Canadian employment agencies. There was no mention of the "Campus Giveaway" allegation that Chinese Canadian students were foreigners displacing "true" Canadians in professional colleges. And there was little mention of the CTV's insensitive stance in the dispute that ensued following the original program.

But by this time anti-*W5* activists were a spent force. Only in Vancouver did "White and Bright" elicit any response. Members of Pender Guy (Pender "guy," or street, is Vancouver Chinatown's main street), a Chinese Canadian radio program on CFRO, argued that it did not "repair the damage done by 'Campus Giveaway.'" Pender Guy called "White and Bright" a "low-budget, low energy production" and asked rhetorically, "Was this a measure of CTV *W5*'s depth of apology?"[56]

These criticisms, however, were simply ignored by the

Toronto-dominated Chinese Canadian National Council for Equality, the Ad Hoc Committees' permanent successor. In time, most of the local chapters outside of Ontario felt alienated from the Toronto group. The CCNCE was becoming an umbrella organization, capable of serving only the interests of the Chinese in one province, not a new problem for Chinese Canadians.

During this period, the CCNCE's leadership had also changed. No longer was it oriented to the grass roots, as was the case during the anti-*W5* campaign. Of the CCNCE's ten directors, only four were active in the anti-*W5* movement.[57]

On March 30, 1981, the CCNCE received a $44,000 operating grant from Ottawa. In the letter to CCNCE president Joseph Wong, the minister of state for multiculturalism, Jim Fleming, remarked that "it is my hope that the financial support provided by the Multicultural Program for your project will enrich the cultural fabric of Canada."[58] The possibility that the CCNCE might direct political dissent toward the government was snuffed out by this grant. This, of course, was not the first time Ottawa had co-opted a potentially critical ethnic organization. In 1969, John Munro and Gerard Pelletier, then, respectively, minister of health and welfare and secretary of state, strongly supported financial aid to the Black United Front of Nova Scotia. Because "agitation which began last fall [1968] has injected into this situation the potential for racial unrest and perhaps violence such as has been seen in similar situations in the United States." Both ministers feared that the withholding of funds would push the black community into the arms of more extreme elements.[59]

Although the CCNCE's politics did not approach the militancy of the Black United Front, it still posed a threat to the Liberal government's multiculturalism policy, particularly if the anti-*W5* forces controlled the CCNCE (the federal grant had the effect of solidifying the organization's conservative element's control). Multiculturalism is the policy of containing French Canadian nationalism by securing support for the government and English power centres among non-British anglophones. The government funded the cultural activities of various ethnic groups and racial minorities (Asians, blacks and natives) but kept them at arm's length from the actual centres of political and economic power. They became, in the words of one critic, "neutralized in their role as providers of individual satisfaction (returning to cultural roots) adding a touch of color to the otherwise drab Canadian sociocultural scene."[60] Multiculturalism became a catch phrase for the government's "increasingly sophisticated strategies for reincorporating potentially dissident groups into the mainstream of society."[61] The CCNCE, a potentially dissident organization, came to the attention of the state as a result of its systematic and well-organized movement against the CTV. Unless properly channelled, such a disciplined and highly motivated group could prove embarrassing to the government. In order to diffuse any future Chinese street campaigns against itself or other important Canadian institutions, the government moved in swiftly with money.

Once the CCNCE came under multiculturalism's umbrella, its campaign for political and economic equality became, by extension, part of the government's own official policy. Though the nub of the agreement was not written down in black and white, the unofficial pact precluded the CCNCE from biting the hand that fed it. What was even more sinister, according to one critic, was that the incorporation of the CCNCE into "the policy of multiculturalism served as a device to legitimize the continued dominance of the ruling English-speaking elite."[62]

Once a strong voice fighting for the rights of Chinese Canadians, the CCNCE quickly withered away when it became part of the cultural limbo of multiculturalism. The final symbol of co-optation, or incorporation into the state structure, occurred during the CCNCE's first annual conference held in Ottawa in October, 1981. While all sixteen local chapters were represented,[63] few delegates had been involved in the anti-*W5* campaign. Many representatives considered the earlier movement as too militant, too radical. Government financial blessing had legitimized the CCNCE with the political power brokers in Ottawa, in their view; it was now safe to jump on the "equality" bandwagon. On the opening day of the conference the CCNCE dropped the "E" (for "equality") from its name, becoming the Chinese Canadian National Council. The new title was a "reflection of the continuing broadening of concerns, objectives, and potentiality of the National Council."[64] One of its first resolutions was to endorse the Liberal government's policy embodied in the Charter of Rights and Freedoms in the proposed new constitution. It was as if delegates considered inequality licked.

The issue of sexual equality, which caused such heated debate during the April, 1980, meeting, was by October considered almost irrelevant by the predominantly-male executive. While $500 was allocated to a subcommittee with the grandiose name of Office of Women Affairs, it was only a pittance in the total budget of $80,000. Such a low budget for feminist issues was a reflection of the leadership's thinking concerning sexism and the status of Chinese women as a minority group within a minority. Instead of pursuing issues of political and sexual equality, the CCNC dedicated itself to gathering historical artifacts about the Chinese in Canada, producing an annual heritage exhibition and festival, establishing a scholarship fund for a deserving student in Chinese Canadian studies, and "promoting co-operation among various ethnic, cultural and civil liberties associations."[65] Its initial *raison d'etre*, to be an advocate for Chinese Canadians, fell by the wayside. Instead, the CCNC became one of many ethnic deputies of the state whose purpose was to keep dissidents in line and to monitor activities of the non-British communities across the country on behalf of the Anglo ruling elite.

## Back to Basics

The conservative drift of the CCNCE was anticipated by a

few Chinese grass roots activists as early as April, 1980. Their perspective on Chinese Canadian politics, developed on the Chinatown streets of Vancouver and Toronto, anticipated divisions. But differences were temporarily set aside in the alliance formed to fight the CTV. When Chercover apologized, and CCNCE leadership was assumed by Hong Kong-born Chinese, the Canadian- and Shanghai-born Chinese quickly returned to their interrupted careers, families and other interests. The CCNCE (and later the CCNC) became just another Chinatown faction in search of government funding.

Whatever its consequences, the anti-*W5* movement brought together broad sectors of the Chinese community in a mission that went beyond the parochial interests of particular factions. Under the leadership of progressive, young Chinese, it represented a moment of solidarity in our history that will serve as a reference point for further actions. It also politicized the works of many Chinese writers in the revitalized Asian Canadian literary scene.

# TOUCHING THE PAST

In 1919, a newly-arrived Chinese immigrant carved this poem on the walls of his cell in the Victoria immigration building:

I have always yearned to go to Gold Mountain.
But instead it is hell, full of hardships. I was
detained in a prison and tears rolled down my
cheeks.
My wife at home is longing for my letter,
Who can foretell when I will be able to return
home?
I cannot sleep because my heart is filled with
hate. When I think of the foreign barbarians,
my anger will rise sky high. They put me in jail
and make me suffer this misery. I moan until
the early dawn,
But who will console me here?[1]

But it was to be another three generations before Asian

Canadian literature, painting, sculpture and other art forms were to flourish. For more than half a century the Chinese struggled to survive in an inhospitable country, their energies channelled into their small shops and cafes, into backbreaking labor in mines and canneries. Not much time was available for the contemplation and reflection necessary for art and writing.

The sons and daughters of merchants were given a practical education. To learn arithmetic so one could maintain an accounting ledger or keep track of inventory—*that* was the purpose of school. Asian Canadians were too busy providing for and protecting their families in a hostile world to have time for art.

The American civil rights movement and black activism was a turning point for Asian-North American culture.[2] The concept of black consciousness electrified the Asian communities on the American west coast; Asians began to demand Asian American studies centres and courses on the experience of Asians in America. Militancy and radicalism characterized the movement. Within a few short years, a string of ethnic studies programs stretched from Seattle to San Diego, concentrating on Asian, black, Chicano and Native American studies. Publications like *Bridge* and *Amerasia* sprang up to meet the needs of the new Asian American sensibility.

The surge of new interest in an Asian American psyche that was neither wholly Asian nor American resulted in a flood of fiction and poetry by writers such as Maxine Hong Kingston, Frank Chin, Jeffrey Chan, Louis Chu, Lawson Inada, Toshio Mori, John Okada and Shawn Wong.[3] In the balance, their works were distinguished by American influences far more than Asian: love and hate in and of America were their themes, and Mailer, Hemingway, Ferlinghetti, Ginsberg and Miller were their inspirations.

Years of neglect, isolation and indifferences had cut off North America's Asians, whose own roots were in the gold rush and railway-building days, from Asian tradition and culture. But white North America's insistence on associating Western-born Asians with a mythological Asia that existed only in their own minds, fostered powerful stereotypes that, ironically, were absorbed even by Asians themselves. Asian children growing up in San Francisco or Victoria learned through Charlie Chan how wise and brilliant the Chinese were supposed to be; Pearl Buck's *The Good Earth* stamped into them the notion that poverty was the result of laziness. Hard work, initiative and resourcefulness became traits associated with the Asian farmer and worker.

The American stereotypes of Asians—Charlie Chan, Mr. Moto, Fu Manchu, the Red Scare, Suzy Wong, Madame Butterfly, David Carradine the little grasshopper, and the sojourner—also had an influence on Canadian children. Asians came to be perceived as having a rich mixture of Eastern and Western culture. Even those Asians whose roots in North America went back as far as 1858 were told they were lucky to possess this "exotic" cultural blend. For the most part, this dual heritage trap was leading many to perceive their identity as split and as imposed against their will. Where they were actually born, and what cultural influences they were really exposed to, mattered little. Even third and fourth generation Asian Canadians continued to be regarded by white society as foreigners, as sojourners. Those Asian Canadians who protested this stereotyping would be patronizingly reassured that "their" Asian heritage was far superior to that of bland, homogenized Canada. Yet for the Chinese, raised on the same diet of Betty Boop, Christianity, Leacock, and the Royal Family as other Canadians, Asian culture was often as foreign to them as it was to whites.

Many Chinese who experienced widespread alienation placed a premium on seeming like the majority. Assimilation—in dress, manners, lifestyle and work ethic—was more than a casual goal of many Chinese Canadians. Many turned their backs on the Asian culture and customs, which were in reality as foreign to them as they were to an Italian, Jew or Briton living in Canada (meanwhile, newer immigrants from Asia sneered at these "Asian whites" for their attitude toward things Chinese). Few Asian Canadians knew much of the colonization of Hong Kong, of Mao Zedong's Long March; they were more at home with tales of Louis Riel's exploits, and of the Winnipeg general strike. Yet Chinese students were denied identification with this history. Racism and bigotry conceded that the only history that was theirs belonged to the country they had left behind.

This contradiction has impressed itself most sharply on Asian Canadian literature of the last few years. Inspired by the Asian American literary movement as well as by the rise of French Canadian nationalism, these Asian Canadian writers have written with an uncompromising honesty about life in a predominantly white country. The satirist Sean Gunn, in a poem called "and then went something," writes:

> click click
> criminal like man with no culture
> very difficult to find true identity
> gee pop
>
> click click
> ancient chinese secret
> calgonite
> click click
> hey chinaman
> hey you
> chinaman
> what are you doing playing these here parts
> I am *bok guey* come
> in search of my long lost
> brother the reason why I shave my head
> is so that I can say
> etcetera etcetera etcetera[4]

He also has this to say about the meaning of the word "Chinese":

in the world today
Chinese
are people
who live
in China

on the local scene
Chinese
are adjectives
that modify people[5]

Mabel Chiu's "Yvonne's Secret" questions what is meant by the same word:

Yvonne has a secret to tell
with a young smile
and hushed voice,

"I'm Chinese."

Yvonne widens her six year old eyes
in wonder
in marvel,

"You knew?"[6]

Much Asian Canadian literature is concerned with the discovery that Chinese Canadians have a cultural identity that is neither Chinese nor Canadian, but *Chinese Canadian*. Stories and poems abound about Asians who return to the homeland of their ancestors in search of their roots, only to discover that their identity cannot be found in Asia after all. This preoccupation with searching for an identity in the country of their ancestors—which is common to many immigrant groups—shows a deep cleavage in the psyche of Asians in Canada. Paul Yee in his story "Prairie Night 1939"[7] and Sky Lee in "Broken Teeth"[8] concentrate on their actual cultural roots: in the small Chinese communities scattered across twentieth century Canada, in the tension between the culture they had left behind and the culture they are trying to adopt. Jim Wong-Chu's "old chinese cemetary (kamloops 1977/july)" reflects this perspective:

> I walk
> on earth,
> above bones of a multitude
> of golden mountain men
> searching for scraps
> of haunting memories.
> like a child unloved
> pressing his face hard
> against the wet window
> peering in
> straining with anguish
> for a desperate moment
> I touch my past.[9]

Another theme in Asian Canadian poetry and fiction is the complete submersion of Asian Canadian history and culture under the dominant European white culture. Eileen Duh's short story "Thought in the Suburbs: The Journey Home,"[10] Sean Gunn's poem "assimilation"[11] and Joy Kogawa's poem "Girls in the Ginza"[12] all talk about this trend, not surprisingly with hostility. In "Fight #Approx.?," Joy Kogawa evoked exploitation of women, especially in the injustices of marriage and its male-dominated structure:

> he's gone curling, he has-
> took himself down to
> where they are, to the
> slab of ice where there
> are stones and brooms
> and dead centres- and left me
> here alone with two
> sleeping kids and the
> warning to be faithful

and lonely as hell-
he could've drawn circles
on me and swept brooms
across my ice brain, slid
stones to a focal point-
here I'm an empty rink
full of circles and arrows
and he's telling me to be faithful[13]

In contrast to the assertions of a woman's place in the world, Rick Shiomi was more concerned with romance and "getting" women. In his story "Akemi," protagonist Ron Tanaka is obsessed with his manhood and the fleeting and incomprehensible virtues of beautiful women. Tanaka remembered that "he had passed through so many women but the mystery of those affairs remained unresolved." Later, he tells Akemi that "I think I have loved and been loved." When Akemi finally rejected him, Tanaka, like a spoiled brat, "packed away his dreams and ran off to Mexico."[14]

Rejection was also the theme of Paul Yee's "Morning Heat." Like Rick Shiomi, Yee's protagonist "meets girl," "loses girl," and pouts. He ended by saying, "Bitch. You could never trust them. They had guys a dime a dozen. But with a body like hers, why not?"[15]

Destroying the image of woman as sexual object, Helen Koyama's "Bar Doors" revealed the other, harder image of Asian woman—the Dragon Lady.

Swinging bar doors part
in fearful respect
she walks in with a dimestore gait
borrowed from a sailor in heat

she is gone
leaving the taste of blood
to linger in their mouths
and they have become no more than olden days
in the memory of this only living being

she is a samurai
and you'd best wipe your feet
and draw your sword
before entering her circle.[16]

On the other hand, intimacy, sensuality, and softness were the major themes of Carol Matsui's poems:

He nuzzles her to
the crazy edge
dabs pine perfume behind her
ringing ears[17]

Until recently, young Asian Canadians were usually shunted into essentially non-verbal and vocational occupations by their high school counsellors and teachers, most of whom were white. This made it difficult for them to develop fluency in English, a circumstance which reinforced their image as being alien and unassimilable. For those young Chinese Canadians with the courage to try their hand at writing in English, the accusation that they wrote "Chinglish" was enough to send them off in search of other endeavors.

For the few who did master English, there were two further obstacles. The first hurdle was to achieve a standard of English acceptable to white critics and readers. Unlike some quarters of the United States where ethnic English has been considered an authentic mode of expression,[18] the English of England was the only yardstick of respectability in Canada. The second problem was the reluctance of publishers and critics to take Chinese authors seriously. In the case of writers concentrating on wholly Canadian themes, a rejection slip might read, "bad syntax and grammar but good content." A common accusation was that the author wrote like a "Chinese" or "Japanese," even though English was their first or usual language of communication.

Largely because of these obstacles, Asian Canadian literature remained stagnant until the 1970s. The sheer size of the Asian population in the United States (about two million) and aggressively obtained government funding for ethnic writers and studies centres gave these writers a new confidence in their work and a recognition of its value from a new generation of readers. American studies programs and centres provided the literary atmosphere and financial stability conducive to research and writing. But in Canada there has never been a single dynamic ethnic studies program for research, writing or teaching.

Asian America provided the model for Asian Canadian writers. It set the pattern for interests and preoccupations. In particular, Asian American writers brought a new pride to being Asian in white America. Inspired by American works, Asian Canadian writers began to celebrate life in Asian Canada. In time, a trickle of poetry and prose began to emerge from Vancouver and Toronto.

As the colony of writers expanded, more Asian Canadians entered the world of literature, drawing courage from the successes of those who had gone before. The literary movement was loosely structured. Its main thematic concerns included exploration of personal and cultural identity, the preservation of ritual, rediscovery of the ancestral homelands, love, hate, assimilation into western culture, and so on. Essentially, the movement rejected stereotypes, ideas and values imposed upon Asian Canadians by white Canada. Its central assertion was that Asians in Canada would be creators of their own histories, culture, mysteries and even their own stereotypes and myths.

Rejection of what was deemed normal and acceptable was the first step toward this renaissance. By challenging the validity of what others thought of their history and culture, these Asian Canadians created an intellectual and spiritual foundation upon which they built their own tradition.

## Literature and History

Celebrating their experiences in poetry and prose and writing their own history was, in part, a process of breaking the paternalistic pattern of relationship between themselves and white Canadians. This relationship, established in the nineteenth century with the introduction of Chinese contract labor into the country's economic system, defined status and power. As "bought" labor, the Chinese were subordinated to the white railway, mine and industrial bosses. Once Chinese labor was no longer useful to an Onderdonk or a coal mining boss like Robert Dunsmuir, it became a floating and potentially troublesome surplus population. Segregated areas like Chinatowns were allowed to exist in order to contain the energies of the Chinese workers.[19]

At the centre of this containment were Chinese merchants who with investments in Canada inadvertently became agents of the government. While the primary purpose of the Chinese Consolidated Benevolent Association, established by merchants, was to fight racism, it also acted as a policing and welfare agency. Merchant interests in the drug trade, gambling, and prostitution kept the workers traumatized or distracted from their social and economic plight.

The strategy of merchant containment of Chinese labor was not without rewards. Merchants were allowed to retain their role as a traditional Chinese gentry with power in the Chinese community. They were also exempted from the head taxes that climbed to $500 in 1904 and which were directed exclusively towards Chinese workers. Their place in Canadian society was ensured as long as they kept to their own ethnic businesses and affairs.

In spite of merchant "arrangements" with the state, racism affected Asian-white relations in social, cultural, educational and political matters. Interracial marriages were frowned upon. The English Canadian view of art and literature was considered the norm. School boards tried to segregate Chinese and white pupils. Asian Canadians could not vote until the late 1940s. A century of unequal treatment nourished the sense of racial inferiority among Asian Canadians. The power structure was based on the supremacy of the white race and subjugation of Asians, blacks and natives. The Asian Canadian literary movement is one attempt to destroy this sense of racial inferiority among Asian Canadians themselves.

# Notes

### Introduction

1. Robert Blauner, "Internal Colonialism and Ghetto Revolt," *Social Problems*, 16 (1968-1969), p. 396.
2. W. Peter Ward, *White Canada Forever* (Montreal: McGill-Queen's University Press, 1978), p. 39.
3. *Report of the Royal Commission on Chinese Immigration* (Ottawa, 1885), pp. *cxxx, cxxxii-cxxxiii*.
4. "An Act Respecting and Restricting Chinese Immigration," Colonial Office to Foreign Office, London, FO 371/8003, June 16, 1922.
5. Peter S. Li and B. Singh Bolaria, "Canadian Immigration Policy and Assimilation Theories," in John Allen Fry, ed., *Economy, Class and Social Reality* (Toronto: Butterworths, 1979), p. 415.
6. Canada, *House of Commons Debates*, 1885, p. 1582.
7. William Lyon Mackenzie King, *Mission to England to Confer with the British Authorities on the Subject of Immigration to Canada from the Orient and Immigration from India, in Particular* (Ottawa: S.E. Dawson, Printer to the King's Most Excellent Majesty, May 4, 1908), p. 7, Sessional Paper #36a cited in FO 228/2237.
8. Canada, *House of Commons Debates*, 1947, p. 2646.
9. British Columbia Legislative Assembly, *Sessional Papers*, 1886, p. 347.
10. Gao Wenxiong, "Hamilton: The Chinatown that Died," *The Asianadian*, I (Summer, 1978), pp. 15-17.
11. Li, "Canadian Immigration Policy," p. 417.
12. Edna Bonacich, "A Theory of Ethnic Antagonism: The Split Labor

Market," *American Sociological Review*, 37 (October, 1972), pp. 547-559.

13. Michael Reich, "The Economics of Racism," in Richard C. Edwards *et al.*, eds., *The Capitalist System*, second edition (Englewood Cliffs, New Jersey: Prentice-Hall, 1978), p. 385.

14. Alan B. Anderson and James S. Frideres, *Ethnicity in Canada* (Toronto: Butterworths, 1981), p. 211.

15. *Ibid.*, pp. 211-212.

16. Ian Roxborough, *Theories of Underdevelopment* (London: Macmillan, 1979), p. 13; Evelyn Kallen, *Ethnicity and Human Rights in Canada* (Toronto: Gage, 1982), pp. 22-24.

17. Edward W. Said, *Orientalism* (New York: Vintage, 1979), p. 206.

18. Ward, *White Canada*, p. 5.

19. Victoria *Daily Colonist*, November 1, 1884.

20. *Ibid.*, September 13, 1907.

21. *Ibid.*, May 2, 1900.

22. Li, "Canadian Immigration Policy," p. 415.

23. Alan Phillips, "The Criminal Society that Dominates the Chinese in Canada," *Maclean's*, April 7, 1962, p. 48.

24. *Ibid.*, p. 40.

25. *Ibid.*, p. 48.

26. Peter Moon, "Assessing Chinese Crime Difficult for Three Forces," Toronto *Globe and Mail*, November 19, 1977.

27. Richard Cleroux, "Montreal Chinatown Tries to Fight a Myth," Toronto *Globe and Mail*, January 2, 1978.

28. "Point by Point Rebuttal of 'Campus Giveaway,'" in Irene Chu, C.K. Fong and May seung Jew, eds., *Living and Growing in Canada: A Chinese Canadian Perspective* (Toronto: Council of Chinese Canadians in Ontario, 1980), p. 125.

29. "Poll finds Support for All-White Society," Toronto *Globe and Mail*, February 27, 1982.

30. Reich, "The Economics of Racism," pp. 387-388.

## Chapter 1: China Roots

1. Edward H. Shafer, *The Golden Peaches of Samarkand* (Berkeley: University of California, 1963), pp. 14ff.

2. Yo K'o, "The Arabs in Canton," in Dun J. Li, *The Essence of Chinese Civilization* (New York: Van Nostrand Reinhold, 1967), p. 324.

3. C.P. Fitzgerald, *China* (New York: Praeger, 1966), pp. 478-479.

4. Teh-ch'ing, "Co-hong Responsibilities," in Dun J. Li, *China in Transition: 1517-1911* (New York: Van Nostrand Reinhold, 1969), pp. 43-46.

5. *Ibid.*

6. Frederic Wakeman, "Canton Trade and the Opium War," in John K. Fairbank, ed., *The Cambridge History of China: Late Ch'ing, 1800-1911*, part 1, vol. 10 (Cambridge: Cambridge University, 1978), p. 204.

7. Jean Chesneaux, Marianne Bastid and Marie-Claire Bergere, *China From the Opium Wars to the 1911 Revolution* (New York: Pantheon,

1976), p. 31.
8. Nicholas Tarling, *Southeast Asia: Past and Present* (Melbourne: F.W. Cheshire, 1966), p. 19; Fitzgerald, *China*, p. 557.
9. Li Zhiqin, "Lun Yapian Zhanzheng Qingdai Shangyexing Nongye Di Fazhan" ("On the Development of Commercial Agriculture in the Qing Era Before the Opium War"), in *Ming Qing Shehui Xingtai Di Yanjiu* (*Studies on the Socioeconomic Configuration During the Ming and Qing Eras*) (Shanghai, 1957), pp. 271, 284.
10. S. Wells Williams, *The Middle Kingdom*, vol. 1 (1899), p. 169.
11. Li Wenzhi (comp.), *Zhongguo Jindai Nongye Shi Ciliao* (*Materials on the History of Modern Chinese Agriculture*), vol. 1 (Peking, 1957), pp. 431-432.
12. Li Zhiqin, "Lun Yapian Zhanzheng," pp. 293-298.
13. E.J. Hobsbawm, *Industry and Empire* (London: Weidenfeld & Nicholson, 1968), p. 28.
14. Wakeman, "Canton Trade," p. 178.
15. Huang Chueh-tz'u, "The Evils of Opium," in Li, *China in Transition*, p. 55.
16. Chesneaux, *China*, p. 55.
17. Harley F. MacNair, *Modern Chinese History* (Shanghai: Commercial Press, 1923), pp. 2-9.
18. Wakeman, "Canton Trade," p. 203.
19. Arthur Waley, *The Opium War Through Chinese Eyes* (London: George Allen & Unwin, 1958), p. 99.
20. Phillip A. Kuhn, "The Taiping Rebellion," in Fairbank, *Cambridge History*, pp. 264-265.
21. Ding Mingnan, et al., *Diguozhuyi quinhuashi* (*A History of Imperialism Against China*) (Peking, 1972), pp. 70-71.
22. Chesneaux, *China*, p. 72.
23. Great Britain Foreign Office, Embassy and Consular Archives, FO 228/61, Enclosure 1, Dispatch 28, February 21, 1846.
24. John K. Fairbank, "The Creation of the Treaty System," in Fairbank, *Cambridge History*, p. 223.
25. Frederic Wakeman, *Strangers at the Gate* (Berkeley: University of California, 1966), p. 131.
26. E.J. Hobsbawm, *Bandits* (London: Weidenfeld & Nicholson, 1969), p. 21.
27. E.J. Hobsbawm, *Primitive Rebels* (New York: Praeger, 1963), chapter 2.
28. Laai Yi-faai, "The Part Played by the Pirates of Kwangtung and Kwangsi Provinces in the Taiping Insurrection," (PhD dissertation, University of California, Berkeley, 1950), p. 6.
29. *Ibid.*, pp. 107-108; Arthur Hummel, *Eminent Chinese of the Ch'ing Period* (Washington: U.S. Government Printing Office, 1943-44), pp. 136-137.
30. *Tanshan Huaqiao* (*The Chinese in Hawaii*), (Honolulu, 1929), section 1.
31. Diane Mei Lin Mark and Ginger Chih, *A Place Called Chinese America* (Dubuque, Iowa: Kendall/Hunt, 1982), pp. 5-6.

32. $US 81 million in gold was extracted. Paul M. Ong, "Chinese Labor in Early San Francisco: Racial Segregation and Industrial Exploitation," *Amerasia Journal* 8 (1981), p. 70.
33. A Chinese account tells of a prospector named Zhang Deming creating the myth of *gumshan*. Mark, *Chinese America*, p. 6.
34. Li Donghai, *Jianada Huaqiao Shi (History of the Overseas Chinese in Canada* (Taibei: Haidian, 1967), p. 60; San Francisco *Globe*, May 16, 1858; Stan Steiner, *Fusang: The Chinese Who Built America* (New York: Harper & Row, 1979), p. 154.
35. Chesneaux, *China*, pp. 90-92a.
36. Vincent Yu-chung Shih, *The Taiping Ideology* (Seattle: University of Washington, 1966).
37. Chesneaux, *China*, p. 96.
38. Cited in Persia C. Campbell, *Chinese Coolie Emigration* (Taibei: Chengwen, 1970), p. 45.

## Chapter 2: Not a Coolie Trade!

1. The Jin was a southern dynasty active during the partition of China along northern and southern lines. Travel from one area to another was therefore from one empire to another. The Jin capital was at Nanjing.
2. *Daqing huitian shili (Precedents and Edicts Pertaining to the Collected Statutes of the Qing Dynasty)*, 1220 chuan (Shanghai: 1899; Taipei: Cheng Wen, 1963), p. 1.
3. *Ibid.*, pp. 1-2.
4. "Qingdai huaqiao zhengce yanbian de jingguo" ("The Process of the Qing Evolutionary Policies Toward the Overseas Chinese"), in *Huaqiao wenti ji (Collected Essays on the Problems of the Overseas Chinese)*, vol. 1 of 7 (Taipei, 1971), p. 108.
5. Campbell, *Chinese Coolie Emigration*, p. 94.
6. Since coolie labor was almost always applied to the West Indies and South America, the jargon of the trade was not used among the Chinese in Canada except for one instance. The Immigration Building in Victoria, B.C., used to house the incoming Asian immigrants, was often called the "pig-pen," or *chu-tsai-uk*, by the Chinese. Chuen-yan David Lai, "A 'Prison' for Chinese Immigrants," *The Asianadian*, 2 (Spring, 1980), p. 17.
7. Campbell, *Chinese Coolie Emigration*, pp. 95-96.
8. Ching Ruji, *Meiguo qinhua shi (A History of American Aggression Against China)*, vol. 1 of 2 (Peking: Sanlian shudian, 1952, 1956), p. 97; Hosea Ballou Morse, *The International Relations of the Chinese Empire*, vol. 2 of 3 (London: Longmans, Green & Co., 1910, 1918), p. 166.
9. Ching, *Meiguo*, 1, pp. 97-98. The Americans were also extremely active in the China-Peru trade. The following is a vivid description of a contract between the Peruvian government and Olyphants & Co. of the United States:
   *Article 3.* This contract is valid for five years only. Within five

years more than 28 coolie shipments should be completed between China and Peru.

*Article 6.* The Peruvian government will not make any coolie carriage contract with any other shipping firm while Olyphants & Co. should proceed to select the best coolies.

*Article 11.* The Peruvian government should pay the said firm $Peruvian 16 million for this service.

*Article 15.* The number of coolies in each shipment should not be less than 500.

Zhu Shijia, *Meiguo pohai huagong shiliao (Historical Materials Pertaining to America's Persecution of Chinese Workers)* (Peking: Zhonghua shuju, 1958), pp. 67-68.

10. Campbell, *Chinese Coolie Emigration,* p. 2n6.
11. Harley F. MacNair, *The Chinese Abroad* (Shanghai: Commercial Press, 1924), p. 211.
12. Ching, *Meiguo,* 1, p. 98.
13. Peter Parker to Daniel Webster, *House Executive Documents,* 34th Congress of the United States, 1st session, vol. 12, no. 105 (Serial 859), May 21, 1852, p. 94.
14. Morse, *International Relations,* 2, p. 167.
15. Campbell, *Chinese Coolie Emigration,* p. 101.
16. *Ibid.,* p. 102.
17. Zhu, *Meiguo pohai,* pp. 35, 17.
18. MacNair, *The Chinese Abroad,* pp. 15-16.
19. Tyler Dennett, *American Policy in China, 1840-1870* (Washington: Carnegie Endowment for International Peace, 1921), p. 137.
20. Zhang Renyu, *Meidi paihua shi (A History of American Imperialism Against China)* (Peking: Wenhua gongyin she, 1951), p. 18.
21. Gerald E. Dirks, *Canada's Refugee Policy* (Montreal: McGill-Queen's University, 1977), p. 25.
22. *Royal Commission, 1885,* p. *xxvu.*
23. *Ibid.,* pp. 192-193.
24. A.W. Loomis, "The Six Chinese Companies," *Overland Monthly,* 1 (September, 1868), pp. 221-227, has a report on the workings of the Six Companies through an "outsider's'" eyes.
25. *Royal Commission, 1885,* pp. 192-193.
26. *Ibid.,* p. 85.
27. Campbell, *Chinese Coolie Emigration,* p. 28.
28. *Royal Commission, 1885,* p. 162.

### Chapter 3: Bachelor Workers

1. *Royal Commission, 1885,* pp. *xxviii, lxxvi,* 46, 161.
2. Harry Gregson, *A History of Victoria, 1842-1970* (Vancouver: J.J. Douglas, 1977), p. 12.
3. Li, *Jianada,* p. 59; Chen Tien-fan, *Oriental Immigration in Canada* (Shanghai: Commercial Press, 1931), p. 33; James Morton, *In The Sea of Sterile Mountains: The Chinese in British Columbia* (Vancouver: J.J. Dougias, 1974), pp. 5-7; G.P.V. Akrigg and Helen Akrigg, *British*

*Columbia Chronicle, 1847-1871* (Vancouver: Discovery Press, 1977), p. 108.

4. Margaret A. Ormsby, *British Columbia: A History* (Toronto: MacMillan, 1971), p. 130.
5. Akrigg, *British Columbia Chronicle*, pp. 119, 115, 165, 247.
6. Gregson, *Victoria*, p. 12; Akrigg, *British Columbia Chronicle*, p. 105.
7. Li, *Jianada*, p. 81; Morton, *Sterile Mountains*, pp. 7-8.
8. Gregson, *Victoria*, p. 21.
9. Victoria *British Colonist*, January 26, 1860.
10. Li, *Jianada*, p. 92.
11. *Report of the Royal Commission on Chinese and Japanese Immigration, Session 1902* (Ottawa: S.E. Dawson, 1902), pp. 12-13, 22.
12. *Ibid.*, p. 65.
13. Robert Edward Wynne, "Reaction to the Chinese in the Pacific Northwest and British Columbia, 1850-1911," (PhD dissertation, University of Washington, Seattle, 1964), p. 145.
14. *Royal Commission, 1902*, pp. 236, 36.
15. Edgar Wickberg, *The Chinese in Philippine Life, 1850-1898* (New Haven: Yale University, 1965); Yen Ching-hwang, *The Overseas Chinese and the 1911 Revolution* (London: Oxford University, 1976).
16. Wakeman, *Strangers at the Gate*, p. 110n.
17. *Journal of the North China Branch of the Royal Asiatic Society* (1865), 2, p. 143; *North China Herald*, April 30, 1864.
18. Ormsby, *British Columbia*, p. 281; Morton, *Sterile Mountains*, pp. 55, 106.
19. Morton, *Sterile Mountains*, p. 94; Li, *Jianada*, p. 127.
20. Victoria *Colonist*, November 15, 1882.
21. Pierre Berton, *The Last Spike* (Toronto: McClelland & Stewart, 1971), pp. 182-185.
22. *Royal Commission, 1885*, pp. 84-85, 149; Gustavus Myers, *A History of Canadian Wealth* (Toronto: James Lewis & Samuel, 1972), p. 270.
23. *Royal Commission, 1885*, pp. 313-314; Ronald T. Takaki, *Iron Cages: Race and Culture in Nineteenth Century America* (New York: Alfred A. Knopf, 1979), pp. 229-230.
24. *Royal Commission, 1885*, p. 71.
25. Cited in Berton, *The Last Spike*, p. 198.
26. Canada, *House of Commons Debates*, 1882, p. 1476.
27. *Royal Commission, 1885*, p. 156.
28. Morton, *Sterile Mountains*, p. 77; Berton, *The Last Spike*, p. 196.
29. Berton, *The Last Spike*, p. 196.
30. *Ibid.*, pp. 196-197.
31. Myers, *Canadian Wealth*, pp. 245-246.
32. Norman Thompson and J.H. Edgar, *Canadian Railway Development: From the Earliest Times* (Toronto: MacMillan, 1933), pp. 138-139; Berton, *The Last Spike*, pp. 196-197.
33. Berton, *The Last Spike*, p. 206.
34. *Ibid.*, p. 213.
35. Morton, *Sterile Mountains*, p. 84; Berton, *The Last Spike*, pp. 200-201.

36. Li, *Jianada*, p. 131.
37. Berton, *The Last Spike*, p. 212.
38. Joseph Krauter and Morris Davis, *Minority Canadians: Ethnic Canadians* (Toronto: Methuen, 1978), p. 61.
39. *Royal Commission, 1885*, p. 366.
40. Berton, *The Last Spike*, p. 204.
41. *Ibid.*
42. *Royal Commission, 1885*, pp. 363-365.
43. Paul Voisey, "The Chinese Community in Alberta: An Historical Perspective," *Canadian Ethnic Studies*, II (1970), p. 18; Ban Seng Hoe, *Structural Changes of Two Chinese Communities in Alberta, Canada*, National Museum of Man, Mercury Studies, Paper 19 (Ottawa: Canadian Centre for Folk Cultural Studies, Paper 19 (Ottawa: Howard Palmer, "Anti-Oriental Sentiment in Alberta, 1880, 1920," *Canadian Ethnic Studies*, II (December, 1970), pp. 31-57; J. Brian Dawson, "The Chinese Experience in Frontier Calgary, 1885-1910," pp. 124-140 in Anthony W. Rasporich and Henry C. Klassan, eds., *Frontier, Calgary: Town, City, and Region, 1875-1940* (Calgary: McClelland & Stewart West, 1975).
44. Interview with Deep Quong, Toronto, Ontario, April 13, 1981; *Project Integrate, An Ethnic Study of the Chinese Community of Moose Jaw*, Report of a Summer O.F.Y. Project, 1973, p. 9. (mimeographed)
45. Julia Kwong, "Transformation of An Ethnic Community: From National to a Cultural Community," in K. Victor Ujimoto and Gordon Hirabayashi, eds., *Asian Canadians and Multiculturalism: Proceedings, Asian Canadian Symposium IV of the Canadian Asian Studies Association*, Universite de Montreal, Montreal, Quebec, May 25 to 28, 1980, pp. 87-88.
46. Lau Bo, "Hostages in Canada: Toronto's Chinese (1880-1947)," *The Asianadian*, I (Summer, 1978), pp. 11-12; Paul S. Levine, "Historical Documentation Pertaining to Overseas Chinese Organizations," (MA thesis, University of Toronto, Toronto, 1975), pp. 78-83; *Royal Commission, 1902*, p. 37.
47. Gao, "Hamilton: The Chinatown that Died," pp. 15-17
48. Ban Seng Hoe, "The Assimilation of the Sino Quebecois," *Chinatown News*, XXVI (August 3, 1979), pp. 5, 25.
49. Lawrence N. Shyu, *The Chinese in New Brunswick*, p. 4. (mimeographed)
50. Interview with Chuck Lee, *Minority Perspective*, Channel 10, Dartmouth, Nova Scotia.
51. Margaret Chang, "Chinese Come to Newfoundland," St. John's *Evening Telegram*, February 11, 1978, p. 17.
52. *Royal Commission, 1885*, pp. *viii*.

## Chapter 4: Bachelor Society

1. *Royal Commission, 1902*, pp. 14-16.
2. Wu Cheng-tsu, *"Chink"* (New York: World, 1972), pp. 70-75.

3. C.E. Trasov, "History of the Opium and Narcotic Drug Legislation in Canada," *The Criminal Law Quarterly*, 4 (1962), p. 275.
4. R.C. Macleod, *The NWMP and Law Enforcement, 1873-1905* (Toronto: University of Toronto, 1976), pp. 124-125.
5. R. Solomon and T. Madison, "The Evolution of Non-Medical Opiate Use in Canada, 1870-1929," *Drug Forum*, 5 (1977), pp. 239-249; Shirley Cook, "Canadian Narcotics Legislation, 1908-1923: A Conflict Interpretation," *Canadian Review of Sociology and Anthropology*, 6 (1969), pp. 36-46.
6. *Royal Commission, 1885*, pp. 369, 150-151.
7. Li, *Jianada*, p. 127.
8. Clyde Brion Davis, *Something for Nothing* (Philadelphia: J.P. Lippincott, 1956), pp. 46-47.
9. *Royal Commission, 1885*, pp. 222-223.
10. *Royal Commission, 1902*, p. 22.
11. Kathryn Warden, "Chinese More Comfortable in Calgary Scene," Calgary *Herald*, March 10, 1979; Emily F. Murphy, *The Black Candle* (Toronto: Thomas Allen, 1922), p. 238.
12. K. Paupst, "A Note on Anti-Chinese Sentiment in Toronto Before the First World War," *Canadian Ethnic Studies*, 9 (1977), p. 58.
13. Cassandra Kobayashi, "Sexual Slavery in Canada: Our Herstory," *The Asianadian*, I (Fall, 1978), p. 7.
14. San Francisco *Chronicle*, 1869.
15. Kobayashi, "Sexual Slavery," p. 7.
16. Li, *Jianada*, pp. 137-144; Nancy Ing, "Beyond Golden Mountain: A Film Diary," *The Asianadian*, III (1980).
17. *Royal Commission, 1902*, pp. 38-41.
18. Lucie Cheng Hirata, "Free, Indentured, Enslaved: Chinese Prostitutes in Nineteenth Century America," *Signs*, 5 (1979), p. 28.
19. *Royal Commission, 1902*, p. 38.
20. *Ibid.*
21. Lai, "A 'Prison' for Chinese Immigrants," pp. 16-19, has the complete information on the "detention hospital" and a list of other poems written by several Chinese immigrants.

## Chapter 5: Banding Together

1. Li, *Jianada*, pp. 132-133.
2. Chuen-yan David Lai, "The Chinese Consolidated Benevolent Association in Victoria: Its Origin and Functions," *BC Studies*, XV (1972), pp. 53-59; Li, *Jianada*, pp. 132, 183.
3. Lai, "Chinese Consolidated Benevolent Association," pp. 57-58.
4. *Ibid.*, pp. 53-59; Li, *Jianada*, pp. 132, 183.
5. Li, *Jianada*, pp. 132-135.
6. Ch'u T'ung-tsu, *Local Government in China under the Ch'ing* (Cambridge: Harvard University, 1962).
7. Philip A. Kuhn, *Rebellion and its Enemies in Late Imperial China: Militarization and Social Structure, 1796-1864* (Cambridge: Harvard University, 1970), p. 120.

8. Stanford M. Lyman, William E. Wilmott and Benching Ho, "Rules of Chinese Secret Society in British Columbia," *Bulletin of the School of Oriental and African Studies*, XXVII (1964), pp. 530-539.
9. Edgar Wickberg, "Chinese and Canadian Influences on Chinese Politics in Vancouver, 1900-1947," *BC Studies*, No. 45 (Spring, 1980), p. 41; Li, *Jianada*, pp. 132, 183; Lai, "Chinese Consolidated Benevolent Association," pp. 53, 56-59.
10. Jean Chesneaux, *Secret Societies in China*, trans. Gillian Nettle (London: Heinemann Educational Books, 1971), pp. 23-27.
11. *Ibid.*, pp. 27-31.
12. Fei Hsiao-tung, *Peasant Life in China* (London: Routledge & Kegan Paul, 1939), pp. 273ff; *China's Gentry* (Chicago: University of Chicago, 1953), p. 233n.
13. *Ibid.*
14. For water rates, gas, and electricity, insurance, and taxes, calculations were arrived at by dividing the amount paid per year by the number of firms (109) in Victoria in 1902 and by twelve months. *Royal Commission, 1902*, p. 212. Other expenses for Ming Lee and Sun San-cheng, see *Ibid.*, pp. 175-176.
15. See Chapter 3, p. 67.
16. All of the works on the Chinese in Canada still retain this outdated notion. The latest in the series of stereotyping is contained in W. Peter Ward, *White Canada Forever*, p. 127, who unequivocally stated that groceries, restaurants, rooming houses, barber shops, laundries and dry-cleaning businesses "were forms of petty commerce which offered services in common demand and required few skills, *low capital investment*, and only a modest knowledge of English." My emphasis.
17. *Royal Commission, 1902*, p. 175.
18. *Ibid.*, p. 180.
19. *Ibid.*, p. 212.
20. Chen Shancheung, "50¢ Special at the Panama," *The Asianadian*, I (1979), pp. 6-8.
21. Gary Coull, "Canada in Asia," *Far Eastern Economic Review*, 112 (June 21, 1981), p. 37.
22. *Royal Commission, 1902*, pp. 212-213.
23. *Royal Commission, 1885*, pp. iv-x.

### Chapter 6: Merchant Society

1. *The Analects of Confucius*, trans. Arthur Waley (New York: Random House, 1938), p. 166.
2. William H. McNeill and Jean W. Sedlar, eds., *Classical China* (New York: Oxford University, 1970), pp. 16-17.
3. *Ibid.*, p. 17.
4. Wing-tsit Chan *et al.*, comp., *The Great Asian Religions* (London: Collier-MacMillan, 1969), p. 125.
5. C.K. Yang, *Religion in Chinese Society* (Berkeley: University of California, 1967), pp. 29-30.
6. Chen, "50¢ Special at the Panama," pp. 7-8.

7. Maurice Freedman, *Chinese Family and Marriage in Singapore* (New York: Johnson Reprint, 1970), p. 128.
8. Chen, "50ᶜ Special at the Panama," p. 7.
9. *Royal Commission, 1902*, p. 33.
10. Mary Ashworth, *The Forces Which Shaped Them: A History of the Education of Minority Group Children in British Columbia* (Vancouver: New Star, 1979), p. 82.
11. *Ibid.*, p. 60.
12. Freedman, *Chinese Family*, pp. 134-136.
13. *Ibid.*, p. 104.
14. *Ibid.*, p. 137.

### Chapter 7: Escape From the Empire

1. Michael Lowe, *Imperial China* (New York: Praeger, 1969), p. 235.
2. Victor Purcell, *The Chinese in Southeast Asia* (London: Oxford University, 1965), p. 24.
3. June Mei, "Socioeconomic Origin of Emigration: Guangdong to California, 1850-1882," *Modern China*, 5 (October, 1979), p. 478.
4. Wakeman, *Strangers at the Gate*, pp. 117-118.
5. Boris Novikov, "The Anti-Manchu Propaganda of the Triads, ca. 1800-1860," in Jean Chesneaux, ed., *Popular Movements and Secret Societies* (Stanford: Stanford University, 1922), pp. 49-63.
6. Chesneaux, *China*, p. 196.
7. Harold Z. Schiffrin, *Sun Yat-sen and the Origins of the Chinese Revolution* (Berkeley: University of California, 1968), pp. 161, 183.
8. Wickberg, "Chinese and Canadian Influences," p. 40.
9. *Ibid.*; Harold Z. Schiffrin, "The Enigma of Sun Yat-sen," in Mary C. Wright, ed., *China in Revolution: The First Phase, 1900-1913* (New Haven: Yale University, 1968), p. 452.
10. Schiffrin, "The Enigma of Sun Yat-sen," p. 469.
11. C. Martin Wilbur, *Sun Yat-sen: Frustrated Patriot* (New York: Columbia University, 1976), pp. 43-44.
12. Li, *Jianada*, p. 302.
13. Chesneaux, *China*, p. 368; Wilbur, *Sun Yat-sen*, pp. 42-43; Yen Ching-hwang, *The Overseas Chinese and the 1911 Revolution* (London: Oxford University, 1976), p. 238; Schiffrin, *Sun Yat-sen*, pp. 138-139.
14. John Fincher, "Political Provincialism and the National Revolution," in Wright, *China in Revolution*, p. 203.
15. Yen Ching-hwang, "Ch'ing Changing Images of the Overseas Chinese (1644-1912)," *Modern Asian Studies*, 15 (April, 1981), p. 284.
16. *Ibid.*, p. 285.
17. Marie-Claire Bergere, "The Role of the Bourgeosie," in Wright, *China in Revolution*, p. 239.
18. Wickberg, "Chinese and Canadian Influences," p. 43.
19. Yen, "Ch'ing Changing Images," p. 282.
20. John A. Macdonald, *House of Commons Debates*, (1882), p. 1476.
21. *Royal Commission, 1885*, p. 41.

22. *Royal Commission, 1902*, p. 65. For more on the "sojourner image," see my "Orientalism and Image Making: The Sojourner in Canadian History," *Journal of Ethnic Studies*, 9 (Fall, 1981), pp. 37-46.
23. Chinese Legation (London) to the Foreign Office (London), Great Britain, Public Record Office, London, Peking Legation Papers, FO 228/2237.
24. Rodolphe Boudreau, "Report of the Committee of the Privy Council, approved by His Excellency, the Governor-General on 31st August, 1980," FO 228/2237. The student tax was later repealed. D. McGillivray to John Jordan, December 21, 1917, FO 228/2676.
25. John Jordan to Foreign Office, March 17, 1909, FO 228/2239. Mackenzie King's Interview with the Acting President of the Waijiaobu, March 9, 1909, FO 228/2237.
26. Mackenzie King's Interview with the Acting President of the Waijiaobu March 9, 1909, Second Interview, FO 228/2237.
27. These figures were contained in a dispatch signed by Mackenzie King. Memorandum respecting the Chinese in Canada. Enclosed in W.L. Mackenzie King to Liang Tunyen, March 11, 1909, FO 228/2237.
28. For more on Yuan's support, see my "Yuan Shih-k'ai's Barbarian Diplomacy," *Asian Profile*, 5 (February, 1977), pp. 9-28.
29. For more on the Reorganization Loan and Yuan's role in it, see my "The Consortium System in Republican China, 1912-1913," *Journal of European Economic History*, 6 (Winter, 1977), pp. 597-640.
30. Li Chien-nung, *The Political History of China, 1840-1928*, trans. Ssy-yu Teng and Jeremy Ingalls, (New York: D. Van Nostrand Co., 1956), p. 286.
31. Chen, "50¢ Special at the Panama," pp. 7-8.
32. Hoe, *Structural Changes of Two Chinese Communities in Alberta*, pp. 182-183.
33. Wickberg, "Chinese and Canadian Influences," p. 44.
34. Lord Devonshire to the Secretary of State for the Colonies, Ottawa, December 29, 1919, FO 228/3103.
35. J.M. Rose-Troup to Miles Lampson, August 17, 1921. Great Britain, Public Record Office, Foreign Office Files, *China, General Correspondence*, FO 371/6584.
36. R. Nathan to Miles Lampson, July 3, 1921, FO 371/6584. For more on the armaments trade and China during the 1920s, see my *Arming the Chinese: The Western Armaments Trade in Warlord China, 1920-1928* (Vancouver: University of British Columbia, 1982).
37. E.D.C. Wolfe, "Smuggled Arms Seized from Ships During 1922," February 12, 1923, enclosed in J.D. Lloyd (Superintendent of Imports and Exports, Hong Kong) to R.E. Stubbs (Governor of Hong Kong), February 30, 1923, FO 228/3108.
38. Lau, "Hostages in Canada," pp. 12-13.
39. Wickberg, "Chinese and Canadian Influences," p. 44.
40. Harold R. Isaacs, *Images of Asia: American Views of China and India* (New York: Capricorn Books, 1962), pp. 164-176.
41. A. Doak Barnett, *Communist China and Asia: A Challenge to*

*American Policy* (New York: Vintage, 1960), p. 1.
42. *Ibid.*


## Chapter 8: Powerless Politics

1. Victoria *Times*, November 14, 1907.
2. See, for example, Patricia E. Roy, "The Preservation of the Peace in Vancouver: The Aftermath of the Anti-Chinese Riots of 1887," *BC Studies*, no. 31 (Autumn, 1976), pp. 44-59.
3. Ken Adachi, *The Enemy That Never Was* (Toronto: McClelland & Stewart, 1976), pp. 95-96.
4. Ward, *White Canada Forever*, p. 37.
5. The best accounts of the 1907 riots are Howard H. Sugimoto, "The Vancouver Riots of 1907: A Canadian Episode," in Hilary Conroy and T. Scott Miyakawa, eds., *East Across the Pacific* (Santa Barbara: ABC Clio, 1972), pp. 92-126 and Adachi, *The Enemy That Never Was*, pp. 63-85.
6. Vancouver *Daily World*, September 9, 1907.
7. W.E. Wilmott, "Approaches to the Study of the Chinese in British Columbia," *BC Studies*, no. 4 (Spring, 1970), p. 47; Edgar Wickberg, "Chinese Organizations and the Canadian Political Process: Two Case Studies," in Jorgen Dahlie and Tissa Fernando, eds., *Ethnicity, Power and Politics in Canada* (Toronto: Methuen, 1981), p. 173.
8. One Japanese was also brought to trial for a concealed weapons offence. The judge admonished him that he was a "poor example" to other citizens. Adachi, *The Enemy That Never Was*, p. 77.
9. Statutes of Saskatchewan, 1912, c. 17.
10. Adachi, *The Enemy That Never Was*, p. 95.
11. Victoria *Colonist*, January 26, 1902.
12. *Ibid.*, January 12, 1922.
13. Ashworth, *The Forces Which Shaped Them*, p. 80.
14. Wickberg, "Chinese and Canadian Influences," p. 51.
15. *Ibid.*
16. Patricia E. Roy, "Citizens Without Votes: East Asians in British Columbia, 1872-1947," in Dahlie, *Ethnicity, Power and Politics*, p. 156.
17. Adachi, *The Enemy That Never Was*, p. 105.
18. Wickberg, "Chinese and Canadian Influences," p. 52.
19. Patricia E. Roy, "The Soldiers Canada Didn't Want: Her Chinese and Japanese Citizens," *Canadian Historical Review*, 59 (1978), p. 341n.
20. Winnipeg *Free Press*, August 21, 1937.
21. Hoe, *Structural Change of Two Chinese Communities*, p. 92.
22. Chuen-yan David Lai, "The Demographic Structure of a Canadian Chinatown in the Mid-Twentieth Century," *Canadian Ethnic Studies*, 11 (1979), p. 50.
23. The best account of the incarceration from an eyewitness view is Takeo Ujo Nakano, *Within the Barbed Wire Fence: A Japanese Man's Account of His Internment in Canada* (Toronto: University of Toronto, 1980). The most recent work from the government's

viewpoint is Ann Gomer Sunahara, *The Politics of Racism* (Toronto: James Lorimer, 1981). For a legal account of the incarcerations and the War Measures Act, refer to Maryka Omatsu, "The War Measures Act: 1914-1979, An Historical Evolution," *The Asianadian*, 2 (Winter, 1979-1980), pp. 19-20.

24. Roy, "The Soldiers Canada Didn't Want," p. 351.
25. *Ibid.*, p. 352.
26. Wickberg, "Chinese Organizations," pp. 175-176.
27. Donald Creighton, *Canada's First Century, 1867-1967* (Toronto: Mac-Millan, 1970), p. 267.
28. Carol F. Lee, "The Road to Enfranchisement: Chinese and Japanese in British Columbia," *BC Studies*, no. 30 (Summer, 1976), pp. 44-76.
29. For examples of anti-Asian sentiments among white Canadians in Ontario, see K. Paupst, "A Note on Anti-Chinese Sentiment in Toronto Before the First World War," pp. 54-59.
30. Lee Wai, in Garrick Chu, *et al.*, *Inalienable Rice: A Chinese & Japanese Canadian Anthology* (Vancouver: Powell Street Revue and the Chinese Canadian Writers Workshop, 1979), p. 30.
31. A. Wei Djao, "Social Welfare in Canada: Ideology and Reality," *Social Praxis*, 6 (1979), p. 39.
32. J.L. Elliott, "Canadian Immigration: A Historical Assessment," in Jean Leonard Elliott, ed., *Two Nations, Many Cultures* (Toronto: Prentice-Hall, 1979), p. 164, Table 2.
33. Freda Hawkins, *Canada and Immigration: Public Policy and Public Concern* (Montreal: McGill-Queen's University, 1972), p. 102.
34. Paul R. Yee, "Where Have All the Young People Gone?" Paper read at the Asian Canadian Symposium V of the Canadian Asian Studies Association, May 24-26, 1981, Mount Saint Vincent University, Halifax, Nova Scotia, p. 4.
35. Patrick Chen, "Chinatown and the Chinese Benevolent Association," in Chu, *Inalienable Rice*, p. 81.
36. *Ibid.*, pp. 81-82; Yee, "Where Have All the Young People Gone?" pp. 4-6.
37. Louis Parai, "Canada's Immigration Policy," *International Migration Review*, 9 (Winter, 1975), pp. 449-477; Richard H. Thompson, "Ethnicity versus Class: An Analysis of Conflict in a North American Chinese Community," *Ethnicity*, 6 (1979), p. 310.
38. Much of the Toronto discussion is from the brilliant study written by Thompson, "Ethnicity versus Class," pp. 306-326. For the section on the new money class and old merchant class antagonism, see pp. 312-313.
39. *Ibid.*, p. 324n.
40. Much of the comments on Chinese women workers in the garment trade is from Winnie Ng, "Organizing Workers in the Garment Industry," *Rikka*, 7 (Spring, 1980), pp. 31-32, 45.
41. Thompson, "Ethnicity versus Class," pp. 313, 319.
42. *Ibid.*

## Chapter 9: Fool's Gold

1. *Inalienable Rice.*
2. *The Asianadian,* I, no. 1 (1978), p. 3; Anthony B. Chan, "Neither French nor British: The Rise of the Asianadian Culture," *Canadian Ethnic Studies,* X, no. 2 (1978), pp. 114-117.
3. "Hong Kong Student Movements and the New Wave of Youthful Thought," *Chishi Niandai (The Seventies),* February, 1980, pp. 65-66.
4. Mary Lee, "Two Cheers for Democracy," *Far Eastern Economic Review,* January 30, 1981, p. 34.
5. For comments on the "cultural baggage" of the Chinese, see "Neither French nor British," pp. 114-117.
6. Aaron Wolfgang and Nina Josefowitz, "Chinese Immigrant Values Changes," *Canadian Ethnic Studies,* 10 (1978), p. 132.
7. See my "The Myth of the Chinese Sojourner in Canada," in K. Victor Ujimoto and Gordon Hirabayashi, eds., *Visible Minorities and Multiculturalism: Asians in Canada* (Toronto: Butterworths, 1980), pp. 33-42.
8. "Point by Point Rebuttal of 'Campus Giveaway,'" in Irene Chu, C.K. Fong and May seung Jew, eds., *Living and Growing in Canada: A Chinese Canadian Perspective* (Toronto: Council for Chinese Canadians in Ontario, 1980), p. 125.
9. *Ibid.,* p. 126.
10. James R. McBride (Executive Director, Canadian Bureau for International Education) to CTV, October 18, 1979.
11. "Point by Point Rebuttal," p. 128.
12. *Ibid.,* p. 128.
13. E.W. Steid, *University Affairs* (December, 1979), p. 2.
14. "Point By Point Rebuttal," p. 129.
15. *Ibid.*
16. Cheuk Kwan, "Media Scare Tactics," *Fuse: The Cultural News Magazine,* IV (March, 1980), p. 133.
17. Donald Chu to the writer, October 4, 1980.
18. Joseph Wong, "Statement from Toronto," First National Meeting of the Ad Hoc Committees of Chinese Canadians Against *W5,* April 18, 1980; Cheuk Kwan, "Political Activism and Chinese Canadians—the *W5* Movement," paper prepared for the 1980 National Conference on Chinese American Studies, October 9-11, 1980, Chinese Cultural Centre, San Francisco, Ca., p. 2.
19. Kwan, "Political Activism," p. 2.
20. The Toronto Ad Hoc Committee was barred from holding its meeting after the initial gatherings. It later held its meeting at the University Settlement House. Deep Quong to the writer, November 1, 1980.
21. "Public Statement Delivered by Dinah Cheng, President of the Association of Chinese Canadian Students and Graduates," November 10, 1979, in *Living and Growing in Canada,* p. 119.
22. V. Carriere, "Court Allows Damages Suit Based on Racial Discrimination," Toronto *Globe and Mail,* December 13, 1979.
23. Andrew Griffith, "Chong Does Wrong," *The Varsity* (University of Toronto), November 3, 1980.

24. Kwan, "Media Scare," p. 144.
25. Angela Christopoulos, "2,000 March on CTV," *The Varsity* (University of Toronto), January 28, 1980.
26. Dick Beddoes, "Tempest Over TV," Toronto *Globe and Mail*, January 28, 1980.
27. Christopoulos, "2,000 March on CTV."
28. Sylvia Stead, "1,500 March to Protest CTV Program," Toronto *Globe and Mail*, January 28, 1980.
29. Beddoes, "Tempest Over TV;" Christopoulos, "2,000 March on CTV."
30. Beddoes, "Tempest Over TV."
31. Christopoulos, "2,000 March on CTV."
32. Beddoes, "Tempest Over TV."
33. Portia Priegert, "Large Turnout for *W5* Protest," *The Gateway* (University of Alberta), January 28, 1980.
34. Paul Clark, "*W5* 'Apology' Rejected," *The Dalhousie Gazette* (Halifax), March 27, 1980.
35. Newsletter of the Ad Hoc Committee of CCCO Against *W5*, Toronto, I, p. 3; Kwan, "Political Activism," p. 6.
36. Newsletter of the Ad Hoc Committee of CCCO, I, p. 3.
37. Nova Scotia Chinese Ad Hoc Committee Against *W5* to the Director (Human Rights Commission, Halifax, Nova Scotia), March 27, 1980; Kwan, "Political Activism," p. 4.

    Earlier examples of political pressure were made in the following: Irene Chu (for the Ad Hoc Committee of CCCO Against *W5*) to J.G. Patenaude (Secretary General, CRTC, Ottawa, Ontario), March 17, 1980; Irene Chu to Dr. Ubale (Ontario Human Rights Commission, Toronto, Ontario), February 23, 1980; Donald Chu to Gordon Fairweather (Canadian Human Rights Commission), January 30, 1980.

    All of these commissions told the ad hoc committees that the *W5* issue "fell beyond their formal jurisdiction." See, for example, Mark Nakamura (Ontario Human Rights Commission) to Irene Chu, March 3, 1980.
38. Helen Hutchinson, "*W5* Statement," March 16, 1980.
39. *Ibid*.
40. The Ad Hoc Committie Against the *W5* Program (Vancouver), Position Paper on the March 16, 1980 Statement by *W5*.
41. *Ibid*.
42. Patrick Ma, Newsletter of Ad Hoc Committee of Chinese Canadians in Edmonton Against *W5*, II, p. 1.
43. Norman Kwan to the author, December 3, 1980.
44. "Chinese Won't Accept CTV Network Apology," Regina *Leader-Post*, March 27, 1980.
45. Mike Boone, "*W5* Adds Whoops to List of Questions," Montreal *Gazette*, April 3, 1980; "Apology Insufficient Says *W5* Ad Hoc Committee," *McGill Daily* (Montreal), April 2, 1980.
46. Clark, "*W5* 'Apology' Rejected."
47. Report from the Tactics and Research Sub-committee, Newsletter of the Ad Hoc Committee Against *W5*, Toronto, II, p. 3.

48. "Text of CTV Statement," *University Affairs* (June/July, 1980), p. 29.
49. Sol Littman, "CTV Apologizes for 'Distorted, Racist' *W5* Show," Toronto *Star*, April 17, 1980.
50. "Two More Quit CTV News Staff," *Globe and Mail*, October 17, 1980.
51. Cheuk Kwan, "The Anti-*W5* Movement," *The Asianadian*, II (Spring, 1980), p. 13.
52. "Proposal from the Working Group of Saskatoon Against *W5*," April 19, 1980; "A Statement by the Chinese Canadian Women's Caucus," April 18, 1980.
53. A. Wei Djao to the author, November 16, 1980.
54. Kwan, "Political Activism," pp. 8-9.
55. Donald Chu to the author.
56. Gordon Chang, "*W5* Settlement Program Aired," *Mainstream*, 3 (February, 1981), p. 29.
57. "Formal Announcement from CCNC," *The Capital Chinese News*, Ottawa, November 1, 1981.
58. Jim Fleming to Joseph Wong, March 30, 1981.
59. Cited in Martin Loney, "A Political Economy of Citizen Participation," in Leo Panitch, ed., *The Canadian State: Political Economy and Political Power* (Toronto: University of Toronto, 1977), p. 456.
60. Karl Peter, "The Myth of Multiculturalism and Other Political Fables," in Dahlie, *Ethnicity, Power and Politics*, p. 57.
61. Loney, "A Political Economy," p. 446.
62. Peter, "The Myth of Multiculturalism," p. 60.
63. Saskatoon, however, was represented by a delegate from Regina.
64. "Formal Announcement from CCNC," p. 18.
65. *Statement of Aims* in Fleming to Wong, March 30, 1981.

## Chapter 10: Touching the Past

1. Lai, "A 'Prison' for Chinese Immigrants," pp. 18-19.
2. "Curriculum Committee Report," *Asian American Review*, Berkeley, 2, (1975), pp. 6-12.
3. Maxine Hong Kingston, *The Woman Warrior* (New York: Vintage, 1977); *China Men* (New York: Alfred A. Knopf, 1981). For other writers, see Frank China *et al.*, *Aiiieeeee! An Anthology of Asian American Writers* (New York: Anchor, 1974), especially pp. ix-xx, 3-54.
4. Sean Gunn, "and then went something," in Chu, *et al.*, *Inalienable Rice*, pp. 56-57. Gunn was born in Vernon, B.C., and is a fourth generation Chinese Canadian poet, Fender bassist and Chinatown political activist.
5. Sean Gunn, "Orientation #1," *Ibid.*
6. Mabel Chiu, "Yvonne's Secret," *West Coast Review*, 16 (Summer, 1981), p. 23.
7. Paul Yee, "Prairie Night, 1939," *Ibid.*, pp. 24-28.
8. Sky Lee, "Broken Teeth," *Ibid.*, pp. 20-23. Lee has also published "Iron Chink: Drawings," *Makara*, 3 (1977); "Gig Goes Island Crazy,"

*The Asianadian*, 3 (Fall, 1980), pp. 10-13; "Sweatshop," *The Asian-adian*, 3 (Fall, 1980), pp. 3-4, also in *Time Capsule*, New York (Spring, 1980).

9. Jim Wong-Chu, "old chinese cemetery (kamloops 1977/july)," *Inalienable Rice*, p. 8. Jim Wong-Chu was born in Hong Kong and was brought to Canada by his aunt as her "paper son." He is a founding member of Pender Guy and has been published in *New Shoots*, (January, 1979), p. 38; *The Asianadian*, 3 (Fall, 1980), pp. 16-17; *West Coast Review*, 16 (Summer, 1981), p. 13. His photos have been shown in *B.C. Photographer*, (Spring, 1975), p. 18; *Inalienable Rice*, pp. 5, 45-47, 81; *The Asianadian*, 3 (Fall, 1980), pp. 16-17; Patricia E. Roy, *Vancouver: An Illustrated History* (Toronto: James Lorimer, 1980), p. 160; and *The Golden Mountain*, Toronto: CBC Film, November, 1981 (stills).

10. Eileen Duh, "Thoughts in the Suburbs: The Journey Home," *The Asianadian*, 1 (Fall/Winter, 1978), pp. 20-23.

11. Sean Gunn, "assimilation," *Inalienable Rice*, p. 44.

12. Joy Kogawa, "Girls in the Ginza," *A Choice of Dreams* (Toronto: McClelland & Stewart, 1974), p. 42.

13. Joy Kogawa, "Flight # Approx.?", *Jericho Road* (Toronto: McClelland & Stewart, 1977), p. 79.

14. Rick Shiomi, "Akemi," *The Asianadian*, 3 (Fall, 1980), pp 5-9. Shiomi has also published "UBC Co-ed Kidnapped," *ibid.*, pp. 26-29.

15. Paul Yee, "Morning Heat," *The Asianadian*, 3 (Fall, 1980), pp. 14-15, 18.

16. Helen Koyama, "Bar Doors," *Inalienable Rice*, p. 68.

17. Carol Matsui, *The Asianadian*, 2 (Winter, 1979-1980), p. 32.

18. For Chinese English in America, see Marjorie K.M. Chan and Douglas W. Lee, "Chinatown Chinese: A Linguistic and Historical Re-Evolution," *Amerasia Journal*, 8 (1981), pp. 111-131.

19. Steven Spitzer describes this containment strategy in "Towards a Marxist Theory of Deviance," *Social Problems*, 22 (1975), pp. 638-651.

# BIBLIOGRAPHY

Anderson, Alan B. and James S. Frideres. *Ethnicity in Canada* (Toronto: Butterworths, 1981). A useful introductory text to ethnicity with some discussion of Canadian racism.

Ashworth, Mary. *The Forces Which Shaped Them* (Vancouver: New Star Books, 1979). The only analysis of the education of Asians, blacks and natives in print. Liberal use of newspaper sources.

*The Asianadian: An Asian Canadian Magazine.* P.O. Box 1256, Station Q, Toronto, Ontario M4T 2P4. Begun in April, 1978, this is the only periodical dealing exclusively with the people of Asian Canada. Focus is on reviews, opinion pieces, people articles (Chinese in Newfoundland, Vietnamese in Sudbury, Koreans in Toronto, Japanese in Greenwood, etc.), fiction, poetry, community reports, overseas Asians, interviews, and a "Dubious Award." Special issues have included "Political Movements" and "Asians in Quebec."

Bolaria, B. Singh. "Cultural Assimilation or Colonial Subordination," in K. Victor Ujimoto and Gordon Hirabayashi, eds., *Asian Canadians and Multiculturalism: Selections from the Proceedings* (Asian Canadian Symposium IV, Universite do Montreal, May, 1980). A conflict approach to the settlement of racial minorities in Canada.

Bonacich, Edna. "A Theory of Ethnic Antagonism: The Split Labor Market," *American Sociological Review*, 37 (October, 1972). Sets the economic problems between white bosses and racial minorities in focus.

Blauner, Robert. "Internal Colonialism and Ghetto Revolt," *Social Problems*, 16 (1968-1969). While it provides an overview of Black

America, it is also useful for analysing Asian Canada. Concise definition of racism.

Blumer, Herbert. "Race Prejudice as a Sense of Group Position," *Pacific Sociological Review*, 1 (Spring, 1958). Contains the essentials for looking at racism as a group threatening process.

British Columbia Legislative Assembly. *Sessional Papers*. 1886-1902. Victoria, British Columbia.

Campbell, Persia C. *Chinese Coolie Emigration* (Taibei: Chengwen, 1970, 1923). One of the first discussions of Chinese emigration to countries of the British empire.

Canada. *House of Commons Debates*. 1882-1886. Ottawa, Ontario.

Chan, Anthony B. *Arming the Chinese: The Western Armaments Trade in Warlord China, 1920-1928* (Vancouver: University of British Columbia Press, 1982). Contains information on "gun-smuggling" from Canada to China by overseas Chinese in Victoria and Vancouver.

_____ "Bachelor Workers in Early Chinese Canada," *Ethnic and Racial Studies*. Forthcoming.

_____ "The Consortium System in Republican China, 1912-1913," *Journal of European Economic History*, 6 (Winter, 1977). Discusses the role of the imperialists on Yuan Shikai's political jockeying with Sun Yat-sen and the Guomindang.

_____ "Neither French nor British: The Rise of the Asianadian Culture," *Canadian Ethnic Studies*, 10 (1978).

_____ "'Orientalism' and Image Making: The Sojourner in Canadian History," *Journal of Ethnic Studies*, 9 (Fall, 1981). Explodes the myth that Chinese immigrants came as transient workers waiting to return to China once their fortunes were made.

_____ "Social Roots of Chinese Emigration to the New World," *Asian Profile*. Forthcoming. Shows the impact of imperialism and rebellion in China on emigration to Canada and the United States.

_____ "Yuan Shih-k'ai's Barbarian Diplomacy," *Asian Profile*, 5 (February, 1977).

Cheng Tien-fang. *Oriental Immigration in Canada* (Shanghai: Commercial Press, 1931). The best analysis in English of Chinese life in Canada by a Chinese citizen.

Chesneaux, Jean, Marianne Bastid and Marie-Claire Bergere, transl. Anne Destenay. *China from the Opium Wars to the 1911 Revolution* (New York: Pantheon, 1976). The best progressive statement on China during the first stages of imperialism and the road to the bourgeois revolution.

Ching Ruji. *Meiguo qinhua shi* (*A History of American Aggression Against China*). 2 vols. (Peking: Sanlian shudian, 1952, 1956). Surveys the history of American imperialism in China from a Marxist perspective.

Chu, Garrick, *et al. Inalienable Rice: A Chinese & Japanese Canadian Anthology* (Vancouver: Powell Street Revue and the Chinese Canadian Writers Workshop, 1979). The best collection of Chinese and Japanese Canadian poetry, fiction, illustrations, opinion pieces and historical articles thus far.

Djao, A. Wei. "Social Welfare in Canada: Ideology and Reality," *Social Praxis*, 6 (1979). A conflict theory approach to the Canadian welfare system.

Fitzgerald, C.P. *China* (New York: Praeger, 1966). Still the best cultural and political introduction to China from the Qin (212-202 BC) to the Qing (1644-1912). Very readable.

Freedman, Maurice. *Chinese Family and Marriage in Singapore* (New York: Johnson Reprint, 1970). Contains much material on Chinese customs and tradition relevent to overseas Chinese communities in other countries.

Great Britain. Public Record Office. Foreign Files. *China General Correspondence*. FO 371, 1912-1928. Contains a wealth of primary material on the Chinese in Canada and other countries of the British empire.

———— *Peking Legation Papers*. FO 228, 1912-1928. Excellent source for research on the Chinese in Canada.

Kallen, Evelyn. *Ethnicity and Human Rights in Canada* (Toronto: Gage, 1982). A useful introductory text to ethnicity with some discussion on Canadian racism.

Lee, Carol F. "The Road to Enfranchisement: Chinese and Japanese in British Columbia," *BC Studies* (Summer, 1976). The only in-depth analysis of the Chinese and Japanese struggle for complete citizenship.

Li Donghai. *Jianada huaqiao shi* (*History of the Overseas Chinese in Canada*) (Taibei: Haidian, 1967). Essential source for any study of the Chinese in Canada. Li was a former secretary of the Chinese Consolidated Benevolent Association in Victoria and is still active in the affairs of the Chinese community.

Li Dun J. *China in Transition, 1517-1911* (New York: Van Nostrand Reinhold, 1969). Excellent compilation of Chinese source material from the Ming to the end of the Qing dynasty.

Loney, Martin. "A Political Economy of Citizen Participation," in Leo Panitch, ed., *The Canadian State* (Toronto: University of Toronto, 1977). An excellent analysis of state co-optation of potentially dissident groups by a well-known student radical who gained fame during the late 1960s.

Morton, James. *In the Sea of Sterile Mountains: The Chinese in British Columbia* (Vancouver: J.J. Douglas, 1974). A classic example of the Chinese-as-victim thesis. Based on newspaper sources, and paternalistic and racist in tone.

Ng, Winnie. "Organizing Workers in the Garment Industry," *Rikka*, 7 (Spring, 1980). The only in depth look at Asian garment workers to date.

Ramcharan, Subhas. *Racism: Nonwhites in Canada* (Toronto: Butterworths, 1982). A slim volume collating minor works of others without much analysis or depth. No theoretical base.

Reich, Michael. "The Economics of Racism," in Richard C. Edwards, *et al. The Capitalist System*. Second Edition (Englewood Cliffs, New Jersey: Prentice-Hall, 1978). An extremely perceptive analysis of racism in the capitalist system.

*Report of the Royal Commission on Chinese Immigration* (Ottawa: n.p.,

1885). Essential primary reading for any work on the Chinese in Canada.

*Report of the Royal Commission on Chinese and Japanese Immigration, Session, 1902* (Ottawa: S.E. Dawson, 1902). Necessary.

Roy, Patricia E. "The Soldiers Canada Didn't Want: Her Chinese and Japanese Citizens," *Canadian Historical Review*, 59 (1978). Excellent in depth analysis of the role of Chinese and Japanese Canadians in the Canadian armed forces during World War II.

————— "'White Canada Forever': Two Generations of Studies," *Canadian Ethnic Studies*, 11 (1979). Surveys works on the study of the Chinese and Japanese in Canada to 1979. Good starting bibliographic essay.

Said, Edward W. *Orientalism* (New York: Vintage, 1979). A brilliant study of Western perceptions of "Orientals," especially people of the Middle East. Contains much that is relevant to Asians in other countries.

Spitzer, Steven. "Towards a Marxist Theory of Deviance," *Social Problems*, 22 (1975). Excellent theoretical analysis of the policy of containment and ethnicity.

Ward, W. Peter. *White Canada Forever* (Montreal: McGill-Queen's University Press, 1978). A scholarly account of Asians-as-victims thesis.

Wickberg, Edgar. "Chinese and Canadian Influence on Chinese Politics in Vancouver, 1900-1947," *BC Studies*, (Spring, 1980). Excellent examination of the political culture of Chinese Canadians.

Yan Gengwang. *Zhongguo difang xing zhengzhi dushi* (*History of the Regional and Local Administrations in China*) (Taibei: Academica Sinica Publications, 1963).

Yen Ching-huang. "Ch'ing Changing Images of the Overseas Chinese (1644-1912)," *Modern Asian Studies*, 15 (April, 1981). Perceptive analysis of Peking's view of the Chinese in other countries from the image of pariah to one of potential financial support.

Zhang Renyu. *Meidi paihua shi* (*A History of American Imperialism Against China*) (Peking: Wenhua gongyin she, 1951). Excellent survey of Chinese-American relations.

Zhu Shijia. *Meiguo pohai huagong shiliao* (*Historical Materials Pertaining to the Persecution of Chinese Workers*) (Peking: Zhonghua shuju, 1958). First study of the overseas Chinese worker within a class analysis.

# Index

*219*

Printed in Canada

**g**